Wintering

By the same author:

The Electricity of Every Living Thing
Burning Out
Ghosts and Their Uses
A Diary of Slow Progress

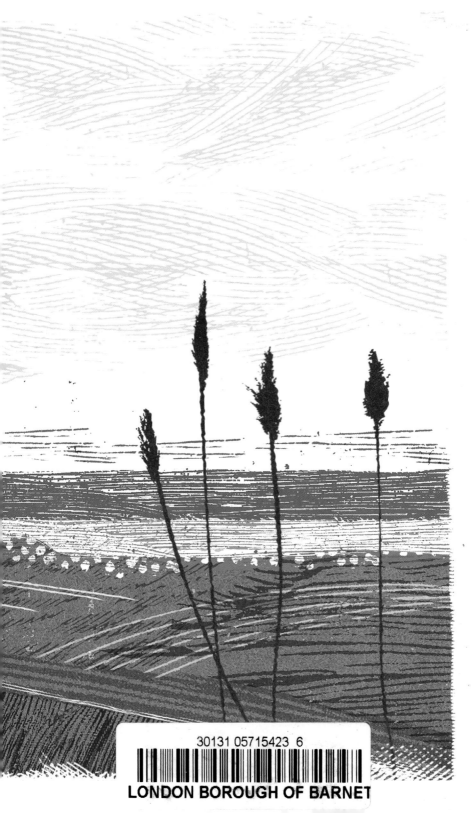

30131 05715423 6

LONDON BOROUGH OF BARNET

Wintering

How I learned to flourish
when life became frozen

KATHERINE MAY

RIDER

LONDON • SYDNEY • AUCKLAND • JOHANNESBURG

3 5 7 9 10 8 6 4 2

Rider, an imprint of Ebury Publishing,
20 Vauxhall Bridge Road,
London SW1V 2SA

Rider is part of the Penguin Random House group of companies
whose addresses can be found at global.penguinrandomhouse.com

Copyright © Katherine May 2020

Katherine May has asserted her right to be identified
as the author of this Work in accordance with the
Copyright, Designs and Patents Act 1988

First published by Rider in 2020
www.penguin.co.uk

A CIP catalogue record for this book is available from the
British Library

ISBN: 9781846045981

Typeset in 13/17.5 pt Bembo
by Integra Software Services Pvt. Ltd, Pondicherry

Printed and bound in Great Britain by Clays Ltd, Elcograf S.p.A.

Penguin Random House is committed to a sustainable future
for our business, our readers and our planet. This book is
made from Forest Stewardship Council® certified paper

Extract from Carol Ann Duffy, 'Prayer', taken from *Meantime*,
copyright © 1993, published by Picador and reprinted by permission of the author.
Extract from Sylvia Plath, 'Wintering', taken from *Ariel*, copyright
© 2015, published by and reprinted by permission of Faber and Faber. Extract from
Eden Phillpotts, *A Shadow Passes* © 1918, published by Cecil Palmer and Hayward.
Extract from Alan Watts, *The Wisdom of Insecurity*, 4th edition copyright © 1987,
published by and reprinted by permission of Rider Books. While every effort has been
made to contact all copyright holders, the author and publishers would be pleased to
rectify at the earliest opportunity any omissions or errors brought to their notice.

For all who have wintered.

CONTENTS

CONTENTS

Over the land freckled with snow half-thawed
The speculating rooks at their nests cawed
And saw from elm-tops, delicate as flowers of grass,
What we below could not see, Winter pass.

Edward Thomas, 'Thaw'

PROLOGUE: SEPTEMBER

INDIAN SUMMER

SOME WINTERS HAPPEN IN THE sun. This particular one began on a blazing day in early September, a week before my fortieth birthday.

I was celebrating with friends on Folkestone beach, the start of a fortnight of lunches and drinks that I hoped would avoid a party and see me safely into the next decade of my life. The photographs I have of that day seem absurd now that I know what was about to happen. High on a sense of my own becoming, I snapped the seaside town bathed in the warmth of an Indian summer. The vintage-looking laundrette that we passed on the walk from the car park. The pastel-coloured concrete beach huts that stack along the Leas. Our combined children jumping over the shingle together, and paddling in an impossibly turquoise sea. The tub of gypsy tart ice cream that I ate while they played.

There are no photos of my husband, H. That's not necessarily unusual: the photos I take, over and over again, are of my son, Bert, and the sea. But what is unusual is the blank in the photographic record from that afternoon until two days later, when there is a picture of H in a hospital bed, trying to force a smile for the camera.

By the time I was taking those idyllic seaside pictures, H was already complaining that he felt sick. It didn't signify much; I have found that parenting a child at infant school brings one long succession of germs into the house, which cause sore throats and rashes and blocked noses and stomach aches. He wasn't even making a fuss. But after a lunch that he couldn't bear to eat, we walked up to the playground at the top of the cliffs and he disappeared for a while. I took a photograph of Bert playing in the sandpit, a rope of seaweed tied to the back of his trousers like a tail. When H came back, he told me that he'd vomited.

'Oh no!' I remember saying, trying to sound sympathetic, while privately thinking what a nuisance it was. We'd have to cut the day short and head back home, and then he'd probably need to sleep it off. He was clutching at his middle, but that didn't seem particularly troubling under the circumstances. I wasn't in any hurry to leave, and it must have shown, because I have a very clear memory of the sudden shock when our friend – one of our oldest ones, known from schooldays – touched me on the shoulder and said, 'Katherine, I think H is really ill.'

'Really?' I said. 'Do you think so?' I looked over to see him grimacing, his face sheened with sweat. I said I'd go and fetch the car.

By the time we got home, I still didn't think it was anything more than a dose of norovirus. H put himself to bed, and I tried to find something for Bert to do, now that he had been robbed of his afternoon on the beach. But two hours later, H called me upstairs and I found him putting on his clothes. 'I think I need to go to hospital,' he said. I was so surprised that I laughed.

We had been through this drill before: two trips to A&E with what might have been a grumbling appendix. Both times the pain had passed. This time it didn't. I dropped Bert off with neighbours and promised to be back in a couple of hours, but soon I was texting them to ask if they wouldn't mind him staying over.

H sat in a plastic waiting-room chair, a cannula in his hand, looking miserable. It was Saturday night: the place was brimming with rugby players admiring their broken fingers, drunks with lacerated faces and elderly people hunched in wheelchairs, their carers refusing to take them back to the residential home. By the time I left him it was after midnight, and he still hadn't been moved to a ward.

I went home and didn't sleep. Returning the next morning, I found that things had got worse. H was vague and hot with fever. The pain had built up through the night, he said, but by the time it was at its peak, the nurses were changing shift, so nobody could give him the medication to make it bearable. Then his appendix burst. He felt it happening. He screamed out in agony, only to be scolded by the ward sister for being rude and making a fuss. The man in the next bed had to get up to advocate on his behalf; he was calling through the curtains to us now, saying, 'Terrible state they left him in, poor fella.'

There was still no sign of an operation. H was afraid.

After that, I was afraid, too. It seemed to me that something dangerous and terrible had happened while I had deserted my post. And it was still happening; the nurses and doctors appeared to be drifting around as if there were no hurry at all, as if a man should lie back and allow his internal organs to rupture without a whimper. I felt, suddenly and furiously, that I could lose him. He clearly needed someone at his bedside to defend him, so that's what I did. I planted myself there, ignoring visiting hours, and when the pain got unbearable, I trailed behind the ward sister until she helped him. I'm usually too embarrassed to order my own takeaway, but this was different. It was me versus them, my husband's suffering versus their rigid schedule. I was not going to be beaten.

I left that evening at nine o'clock, and called every hour until he was safely in theatre. I didn't care that I was being a nuisance. Then I lay awake until he was out again, and I'd heard that he was comfortable. Then I couldn't sleep anyway. At moments like this, sleep feels like falling; you sink into luxurious blackness only to jolt awake again, staring around at the darkness as if you might divine something in the grainy night. The only things I could find were my own fears: the unbearable fact of his suffering, and the terror of being left to survive without him.

I took compassionate leave from work, and kept up my vigil all week between school drop-offs and collections. I was there for the surgeon explaining the extent of the infection with something approaching awe; I was there to fret over H's temperature refusing to fall, his blood oxygen levels failing to return to normal. I helped him to take slow walks around the ward, and watched him sleep afterwards, sometimes drifting off mid-sentence. I changed him into clean clothes, and brought him tiny quantities of food to eat. I tried to soothe Bert's fear of his father, suddenly hooked up to so many wires and tubes and bleeping machines.

Somewhere in the middle of this catastrophe, a space opened up. There were hours spent driving from home to the hospital, from hospital to home; sitting by the side of H's bed while he dozed; waiting in the canteen while the ward rounds took place. My days were simultaneously tense and slack: I was constantly required to be somewhere and awake and vigilant; but I was also redundant, an interloper. I spent a lot of time staring around me, wondering what to do, my mind churning to categorise these new experiences, to find a context for them.

And in all that space it suddenly seemed inevitable that this would happen. A strange, irresistible hurricane was already blasting through my life anyway, and this was just another part of its wake. Only a week ago, I had given notice on job as a university lecturer, trying to find a better life outside the perpetual stress and noise of the contemporary university. I had just published my first book in six years, and had another imminent deadline. My son had only recently returned to school after the long summer holiday, and I had all the usual maternal worries about his ability to step up to the challenges of Year One. Change was already happening, and here was its cousin, mortality, not so much knocking on my door as kicking it down like some particularly brutal extrajudicial force.

I have long told the story of how I managed to gatecrash a wake on my thirtieth birthday. I had arranged to meet a friend at a pub, and blundered my way in to find that it had been booked out to host the aftermath of an Irish funeral. The whole room was dressed in black and a band was playing in the corner, two young women on fiddles, singing folk songs. I should, of course, have turned around and walked out, but I was worried that my friend wouldn't find me then, and it was raining outside. I thought I might just lurk near the door and try to pass unnoticed. Actually, I don't know what I was thinking; any sensible person would have left and sent a text. But I stayed and thought this was just my luck – some kind of harbinger of death to mark the end of my youthful twenties.

The situation only worsened when my friend arrived, and it suddenly became clear that she bore a remarkable resemblance to one of the women in the band, which had now stopped playing. This wasn't just my own view; it seemed that the family of the deceased had mistaken her for the now-vanished fiddler. My friend was hugged and hand-shaken and back-patted, and it was positively insisted upon that she stayed for a drink. Having no idea what on earth was happening, and assuming, I later learned, that this was just the warm hospitality of the Irish, she agreed, and even managed to field questions about her musical talent with what looked like modesty, but was actually flat denial. We only managed to leave because we had theatre tickets that could irrefutably prove we ought to be elsewhere.

The whole episode had the air of a Shakespearean farce, staged just for me. But in retrospect, it was light relief. I passed the cusp of my fortieth birthday with H freshly out of hospital, and all my celebrations cancelled. At ten in the evening, Bert called me upstairs and promptly vomited all over me. He carried on well into the night. But by then, it didn't matter, because I had given up on sleep anyway. Something had already shifted.

There are gaps in the mesh of the everyday world, and sometimes they open up and you fall through them into Somewhere Else. Somewhere Else runs at a different pace to the here and now, where everyone else carries on. Somewhere Else is where ghosts live, concealed from view and only glimpsed by people in the real world. Somewhere Else exists at a delay, so that you can't quite keep pace. Perhaps I was already teetering on the brink of Somewhere Else anyway; but now I fell through, as simply and discreetly as dust sifting between the floorboards. I was surprised to find that I felt at home there.

Winter had begun.

★

Everybody winters at one time or another; some winter over and over again.

Wintering is a season in the cold. It is a fallow period in life when you're cut off from the world, feeling rejected, sidelined, blocked from progress, or cast into the role of an outsider. Perhaps it results from an illness; perhaps from a life event such as a bereavement or the birth of a child; perhaps it comes from a humiliation or failure. Perhaps you're in a period of transition, and have temporarily fallen between two worlds. Some winterings creep upon us more slowly, accompanying the protracted death of a relationship, the gradual ratcheting up of caring responsibilities as our parents age, the drip-drip-drip of lost confidence. Some are appallingly sudden, like discovering one day that your skills are considered obsolete, the company you worked for has gone bankrupt, or your partner is in love with someone new. However it arrives, wintering is usually involuntary, lonely and deeply painful.

Yet it's also inevitable. We like to imagine that it's possible for life to be one eternal summer, and that we have uniquely failed to achieve that for ourselves. We dream of an equatorial habitat, forever close to the sun; an endless, unvarying high season. But life's not like that. Emotionally, we're prone to stifling summers and low, dark winters, to sudden drops in temperature, to light and shade. Even if, by some extraordinary stroke of self-control and good luck, we were able to keep control of our own health and happiness for an entire lifetime, we still couldn't avoid the winter. Our parents would age and die; our friends would undertake minor acts of betrayal; the machinations of the world would eventually weigh against us. Somewhere along the line, we would screw up. Winter would quietly roll in.

I learned to winter young. As one of the many girls of my age whose autism went undiagnosed, I spent a childhood permanently out in the cold. At seventeen, I was hit with a bout of depression so hard that it immobilised me for months. I was convinced that I would not survive it. I was convinced that I didn't want to. But somewhere there, in the depths, I found the seed of a will to live, and its tenacity surprised me. More than that: it made me strangely optimistic. Winter had blanked me, blasted me wide open. In all that whiteness, I saw the chance to make myself new again. Half-apologetic, I started to build a different kind of a person: one who was rude sometimes and who didn't always do the right thing, and whose big, stupid heart made her endlessly seem to hurt, but also one who deserved to be here, because she now had something to give.

For years, I would tell it to anyone who would listen: 'I had a breakdown when I was seventeen.' Most people were embarrassed to hear it, but some were grateful to find a shared thread in their story and mine. Either way, I felt with great certainty that we should talk about these things, and that I, having learned some strategies, should share them. It didn't save me from another dip and another dip, but each time the peril became less. I began to get a feel for my winterings: their length and breadth, their heft. I knew that they didn't last forever. I knew that I had to find the most comfortable way to live through them until spring.

I was always aware that I was flying in the face of polite convention in doing this, and that the times when we fall out of everyday life remain taboo. We're not raised to recognise wintering, or to acknowledge its inevitability. Instead, we tend see it as a humiliation, something that should be hidden from view lest we shock the world too greatly. We put on a brave public face and grieve privately; we pretend not to see other people's pain. We treat each wintering as an embarrassing anomaly that should be hidden or ignored. This means we've made a secret of an entirely ordinary process, and have thereby given those who endure it a pariah status, forcing them to drop out of everyday life in order to conceal their failure. Yet we do this at a great cost. Wintering brings about some of the most profound and insightful moments of our human experience, and wisdom resides in those who have wintered.

In our relentlessly busy contemporary world, we are forever trying to defer the onset of winter. We don't ever dare to feel its full bite, and we don't dare to show the way that it ravages us. A sharp wintering, sometimes, would do us good. We must stop believing that these times in our life are somehow silly, a failure of nerve, a lack of willpower. We must stop trying to ignore them or dispose of them. They are real, and they are asking something of us. We must learn to invite the winter in.

That's what this book is about: learning to recognise the process, engage with it mindfully, and even to cherish it. We may never choose to winter, but we can choose *how*.

*

Our knowledge of winter is a fragment of childhood, almost innate: we learn about it in the surprising cluster of novels and fairy tales that are set in the snow. All the careful preparations that animals make to endure the cold, foodless months; hibernation and migration, deciduous trees dropping leaves. This is no accident. The changes that take place in winter are a kind of alchemy, an enchantment performed by ordinary creatures to survive: dormice laying on fat to hibernate; swallows navigating to South Africa; trees blazing out the final weeks of autumn. It is all very well to survive the abundant months of the spring and summer, but in winter, we witness the full glory of nature flourishing in lean times.

Plants and animals don't fight the winter; they don't pretend it's not happening and attempt to carry on living the same lives that they lived in the summer. They prepare. They adapt. They perform extraordinary acts of metamorphosis to get them through. Winter is a time of withdrawing from the world, maximising scant resources, carrying out acts of brutal efficiency and vanishing from sight; but that's where the transformation occurs. Winter is not the death of the life cycle, but its crucible.

Once we stop wishing it were summer, winter can be a glorious season when the world takes on a sparse beauty, and even the pavements sparkle. It's a time for reflection and recuperation, for slow replenishment, for putting your house in order.

In this book, I set out to understand winter by talking to those who know it intimately: the Finns who start preparing to winter in August, for example; or the people of Tromsø in Norway who don't see the sun from November to January. I will meet people who have lived through illness, failure, isolation and despair, and have come out renewed, and the people who work most closely with the brutal processes of the natural world. I'll explore how to prepare for winter, how to endure its bleakest days, and, finally, how to emerge again into the spring.

Doing those deeply unfashionable things – slowing down, letting your spare time expand, getting enough sleep, resting – are radical acts these days, but they are essential. This is a crossroads we all know, a moment when you need to shed a skin. If you do, you'll expose all those painful nerve endings, and feel so raw that you'll need to take care of yourself for a while. If you don't, then that old skin will harden around you.

It's one of the most important choices you'll ever make.

OCTOBER

MAKING READY

I AM BAKING BAGELS. OR rather, I'm failing spectacu-
larly at it.

The recipe I'm using stipulates a hard dough,
which was all very well until something snapped in
my mixer, making it suddenly scream as though I'd
injured it. Not to be put off, I turned out the dough
onto my kitchen worktop and kneaded it by hand for
ten minutes, put it in an oiled bowl and then left it
to rise in the warm spot that the cat favours on the
living-room floor, where the central heating pipes are
near the surface.

An hour later, nothing seemed to have happened,
so I left it for an hour more before losing all patience
at its unresponsiveness, and shaping it into little rings
anyway. It is only after I have poached them (watching
helplessly as they unravel into weird croissant shapes),
and put them into a hot oven, that I think to check

the expiry date on the tin of yeast I used: January 2013. Five years ago. I suspect I bought it before my son was born, when I last had time to contemplate the production of leavened goods.

The bagels are, unsurprisingly, inedible. No matter. I am not baking because I'm hungry; I am baking to keep my hands moving. Granted, the bagels weren't meant to be quite so hard (both in terms of texture and difficulty), but they have nevertheless filled a gaping hole in my day where work should have been, and making them has staved off looking into the void, at least for a while.

H is now home, and safe, and has even returned to his job. I am heading in the opposite direction. Having rumbled along on high for years now, my stress level has reached a kind of crescendo. I feel physically unable to go into work, as though I'm connected to the house by a piece of elastic that pings me back indoors whenever I attempt my commute. It is more than a mere whim; it is an absolute bodily refusal. I've been pushing through this for a long time now, but something has finally snapped. Perhaps literally. While H was in hospital, I began to notice a grumbling pain along the right-hand side of my abdomen, which I assumed to be sympathetic to his appendicitis. But then it carried on, and in fact seemed to get worse as he got better. He's now happily back at work, a little sore, but largely back to normal. Meanwhile, I have been wincing at the lightest effort. A week ago, I found myself doubled up over my desk, unable to think about anything except the pain I was in. I took the bus home, and I've pretty much stayed here ever since.

I endured a squirming conversation with my GP in which I admitted that I've been studiously ignoring all the major signs of bowel cancer for about a year, and was referred for urgent tests and signed off sick. I can't help but feel that I let the stress run so far out of control that it has begun to eat away at me; that I should have asked for help sooner. But then stress is a shameful thing, a proclamation of my inability to cope. I am slyly pleased that I have pain to contend with, rather than a more nebulous sense of my own over-whelmedness. It feels more concrete somehow. I can hide behind it and say, *See, I am not unable to manage my workload. I am legitimately ill.*

I now have hours and hours of open time to wonder about all these things, and my brain is too foggy to concentrate on much else. I've cooked a great deal since I've been ill. It's a nice, small parcel of activity, just enough for me to manage at the moment. It's not as though cooking is new to me; I have always been a cook. But in the last few years, it has been pushed out of my life, along with its accompanying pleasure of shopping for ingredients. Life has been busy, and in the general rush of things, these vital fragments of my identity have been squeezed out. I have missed them, but in a shrugging kind of way. What can you do when you're already doing everything?

The problem with 'everything' is that it ends up looking an awful lot like nothing: just one long haze of frantic activity, with all the meaning sheared away. Time has passed so quickly while I have been raising a child and writing books and working a full-time job that often sprawls into my weekends, that I can't quite account for it. The preceding years are not a blank exactly, but they're certainly a blur, and one that's strangely devoid of meaning, expect for a clawing sense of survival. Turning over the yeast tin in my hands, I'm struggling to construct an account of myself that gets me from there to here. I feel as though I've been falling down an impossibly long elevator shaft, and have just landed at the bottom with a bump. It's spacious and echoing in here, and I'm still not quite sure how to get out. I'm trying to find my way back to something I recognise.

In Tove Jansson's *Moominland Midwinter*, Moomintroll accidentally wakes from hibernation too early. Accustomed to sleeping through winter, he is shocked to find the world shrouded in snow, his garden entirely unfamiliar. 'All the world has died while I slept,' he thinks. 'It isn't made for Moomins.' Feeling terribly lonely, he goes to the bedroom and pulls back his mother's quilt: 'Wake up! Wake up!' he shouts. 'All the world's got lost!' His mother curls up on her bed-mat, and sleeps on. This is a mirror of my own winter, or how it seems to me: everybody else is drowsing while I am wide awake and hounded by sharp fears.

At these moments in life, you have to keep moving somehow. I'm taking a slow, painful walk every day to the local shops to pick up a few ingredients. My fridge, until recently stuffed full of food that I ordered online and would never quite get around to eating, is currently empty. I'm only buying what I need; I'm ashamed of the waste that I'd accepted as inevitable until recently. But this is the difference that time makes: I can afford the short limp to the high street to see what's piled up in the greengrocer's shop today. If I run out of bread, I can buy some. The butcher can sell me exact quantities of meat, which I know I will use that same day. I no longer have to act out the cycle of freezing a packet of chicken, defrosting it a week later, then not having time to eat it and so throwing it away.

I feel as though I'm cooking autumn into my house. This week, I braised a hotpot with lamb, carrots and thyme, and discs of potato on top. I bought a box of delicately bloomed figs in cerise papers, and ate them chopped on porridge on three successive mornings. I made a velvety soup from a pale green pumpkin, and cured a fillet of salmon with salt, sugar, dill and beetroot, giving it a bright red coat. As an afterthought, I pick-led some ridge cucumbers to go with it. I had time. It was all possible, and all worthwhile.

I've also been enjoying the good set of colouring pencils that I bought for Bert, German ones called Lyra like the ragamuffin heroine of Philip Pullman's *His Dark Materials* trilogy. They're densely pigmented and waxy, a far cry from the cheap ones we normally pick up without thinking, and they've changed the way he draws, making me want to join in. I've almost forgiven them for their eye-watering price: they've outlasted all the others by a country mile.

I had no idea how much these quiet pleasures had retreated from my life while I was rushing around, and now I'm inviting them back in: still, rhythmic work with the hands, the kind of light concentration that allows you to dream, and the sense of a kindness done in the process. I make gingerbread men with Bert and find myself taking excessive care over them, as if they are reverse voodoo dolls. I imagine each one of them as a small act of defiance against the life I've been living. It's a kind of sympathetic magic to handle something so pointless with such reverence: I am tending to the dead, gently laying to rest a set of values for which I no longer have any use.

We bring light into the house in the winter to repel the multiple darknesses that lurk there. I raid the cupboards for candles and hang fairy lights in the murkier corners, and as I do so I start to retell my own story, if only to myself. That's what humans do: we make and remake our stories, abandoning the ones that no longer fit and trying on new ones for size. I am now telling myself the story of a pattern of work that I fell into by mistake, because I was afraid that I would never find my feet again after I had my son. I didn't cope when I was pregnant, I didn't cope when I had a baby, and I started working again to try to swim my way back to dry land. It didn't solve everything, but it gave me back one area of my life in which I felt effective.

I worked all day, and wedged in 5am shifts and the odd hour between nine and ten at night just before I flopped into bed, nearly asleep before my head hit the pillow. I snatched time at weekends to mark papers and write course guides, whenever I could persuade my husband and son to do something without me. People admired me for how much I got done. I lapped it up, but felt, secretly, that I was only trying to keep pace with everyone else, and they seemed to be coping far better. After all, I had colleagues who regularly replied to emails after midnight, long after I was asleep. In actual fact, I was ashamed. I always thought that I, so very wise, would never succumb to work addiction. But here I am, having worked so hard, and for so long, that I've made myself sick. And, worst of all, I've nearly forgotten how to rest.

I'm tired, inevitably. But it's more than that. I'm hollowed out. I'm tetchy and irritable, constantly feeling like prey, believing that everything is urgent and that I can never do enough. And my house – my beloved home – has suffered a kind of entropy in which everything has slowly collapsed and broken and worn out, with detritus collecting on every surface and corner, and I have been helpless in the face of it.

Since being signed off sick, I've been forced to lean back on the sofa and stare at the wreckage for hours at a time, and wonder how the hell it got so bad. There's not a single soothing place left in the house, where you can rest a while without being reminded that something needs to be mended or cleaned. The windows are clouded with the dusty veil of a hundred rainstorms. The varnish is wearing from the floorboards. The walls are dotted with nails that are missing their pictures, or holes that should be filled and painted over. Even the television hangs at a drunken angle. When I stand on a chair and empty the top shelf in the wardrobe, I find that I have meant to replace the bedroom curtains at least three times in the last few years, and every bundle of fabric I've bought has ended up folded neatly and stowed away, entirely forgotten.

That I'm only noticing these things now that I'm physically unable to remedy them feels like the kind of exquisite torture devised by vengeful Greek gods. But here it is: my winter. It's an open invitation to transition into a more sustainable life and to wrest back control over the chaos I've created. It's a moment when I have to step into solitude, and into contemplation. It's also a moment when I have to walk away from old alliances, to let the strings of some friendships fall loose, if only for a while. It's a path I've walked over and over again in my life, perhaps. I have learned how to winter the hard way. It's a skillset, of sorts.

If I didn't see my winter coming, then at least I have caught it in the early stages. I am just a little lost, that's all; just a little clouded over, like my windows. I'm determined to go into it consciously, to make it a kind of practice in understanding myself better. I want to avoid making the same mistakes again. I am almost wondering whether there could be a pleasure in it, somewhere, if only I'm well enough prepared. I can feel the downturn coming; I know that baking and soup-making can't sustain me forever. It will get worse than this: darker, leaner, lonelier. I want to lay down a bed of straw beneath me to cushion the blow when it comes. I want to make everything ready.

★

A windfall of quinces arrives in a carrier bag, sent by a friend who says her tree has cropped like never before this year. I'm not sure when these things are set in train, whether we had a particularly fertile spring, or a summer that maintained exactly the right balance of wet and dry, but my own greengage tree has been abundant too for the first time in the nine years since we planted it. Out on the path along the seafront, the brambles are laden with blackberries and the hedgerows are dotted with bright red rosehips like Chinese lanterns. The summer scatters gifts in its death throes.

My mother is a habitual preserver, and I've inherited a little of that instinct too. We used to descend on my aunt's garden once a year to raid damsons, Bramleys, plums and mulberries, we women all chattering together, our fingers stained with juice. The spoils would be converted into jams and apple chutney in my grandma's wide-mouthed preserving pan, which I still own. My granddad pickled his home-grown shallots, too, and my mum made jars of bright yellow piccalilli and cerise red cabbage. These would all be saved until Christmas, when they would be decanted into bowls for Boxing Day lunch.

There's an unspoken rule to our preserving: you shouldn't have paid for the main ingredient. It should be part of a glut, otherwise unwanted or impossible to use; or should be foraged from the wild, where it would only decay without your intervention. You don't have to look back many generations to see how this was an essential supplement to scarce fresh produce in winter months, although today it's perhaps more of an affectation, an aspect of my personal culture that I'm reluctant to concede. I knock out the occasional jar of chutney, although I rarely have the time for all that chopping and stirring, the sterilising of jars, and I have no love for the offensive smell of vinegar and raw onion that lingers in the house for days afterwards.

No, my urge to preserve takes a far less practical guise. For a start, I tend only to preserve things that I'm curious about, just see what happens. This year, I have pickled a Japanese mooli radish, which I found reduced to 10p at the supermarket and couldn't resist; a miniscule crop of cucamelons that clung to life, un-watered, in a pot on my patio; and a couple of handfuls of marsh samphire, gathered on a walk in a kind of desperate, excited frenzy. I have no use for any of these things, and am likely to watch them all turn slowly grey in their jars before I throw them out. I mainly seem to want to pickle unappetising things. I recently found myself gazing hungrily at a recipe for pickling ash keys, the woody seeds of the tree that overhangs my garden.

Even worse, my favourite preserving medium is alcohol. I have a habit of spending a small fortune on industrial quantities of gin in which to douse windfalls of damsons, elderberries or sloes. The fruit may be free, but the result is an ill-concealed extravagance, particularly seeing as I don't have much of a sweet tooth. I now have an archive of sloe gin going back several years in my wine rack under the stairs. I swear I'll remember to foist it upon visitors at some point.

I consider making a liqueur of the quinces, but I decide, on balance, to turn them into membrillo instead, that dense Spanish jelly that sings with pork and Manchego cheese. I pare off their knobbly yellow skins, dice the pinkish flesh and boil them down into a thick burgundy paste, which spits bad-temperedly as it simmers, threatening to scald my arms. When it's set, I slice it and take a parcel of it to my friend Hanne Mällinen-Scott, hoping she'll be impressed. Hanne is Finnish and another innate pickler. She is intimate with winter; it's in her blood. She rarely misses an opportunity to contrast her Nordic hardiness with our pitiable English frailty.

I tell her about my desire to prepare for a wintering. 'My mother has a word for what you're doing,' she says: '*talvitelat*.' It doesn't quite have an English equivalent, but it roughly translates as being stowed away for winter. 'We used to use it when we put all the summer clothes away and got the winter ones out. It was always a good moment, to see them again. Like having new clothes twice a year.'

'Do you actually do it like that?' I say. 'I mean, you don't just throw on an extra jumper over your normal clothes?'

'No,' says Hanne. 'You can't do that in Finland. The winter arrives very suddenly, and you don't mess with it. You need a completely different wardrobe; you can't just make do. You see people over here acting like winter isn't happening – like those men who wear shorts through December as if they're trying to impress someone.'

'Or the girls who go to night clubs with bare legs and no coat,' I say.

'Right,' says Hanne. 'All they're proving is that it doesn't get very cold in England. I'd like to see them try that shit in Finland.'

Hanne is from Liminka, where the average temperature is 2°C. In July it can soar towards 30°C, but nearly half the year is spent below zero, getting down to −10°C in January. You have to be ready for that sort of winter.

'When do you start preparing?'

'August,' she says, without blinking.

'*August?*'

'More like July actually. You have to get everything done before it starts getting cold. After that, you might not be able to go anywhere.'

'What on earth can you do that early?'

'Well,' she says, 'you make sure that any repairs are done to the house, because snow will only make it worse. No leaks in the roof, that sort of thing.'

'Lag the pipes,' I say.

'Our pipes are underground. Lagging would be useless in Finland.'

'Oh,' I say, 'right.' I'm getting the sense that I wouldn't last out September, let alone make it to February.

'You chop firewood and stack it up properly. You buy winter tyres for your car. You bake so that the freezer is full, because if anyone drops by you have to serve them coffee and cake. That's important: you're always ready to give hospitality. And of course you go out foraging.'

At this thought, Hanne's eyes light up. Like many northern populations, the Finns are expert picklers and preservers, their winter cuisine centring on food that can be stored. Hanne remembers those summer expeditions to pick berries and mushrooms as the high point of her year, when the whole family would set out together with sandwiches, and spend the day picking whatever they could find. It was bonding time, the whole extended clan working together; she even remembers her great-granny coming along to join in.

'My favourites were the milkcap mushrooms,' she says. 'You had to boil them in three changes of salt water to get rid of the poison.'

'How on earth did anyone get around to thinking they were food in the first place?'

'They taste amazing,' she says. 'I think our ancestors probably persevered until we didn't die of eating them.'

'Does it get very dark in the winter?' I ask.

'Yes. I mean, it's not like we're in the Arctic Circle; we still see the sun every day. But there isn't much daylight, and it's bitterly cold outside, so you're forced to adapt. You sleep more, for a start. You can't help it. Your body clock changes; it all balances out across the year. It's true what they say about washing your car at midnight in the summer. In winter, you have to find ways to keep cosy, to make the house cheerful. Otherwise ... ' She pauses. 'People aren't always prepared for the change in their habits.'

'Don't you have the highest suicide rate in the world?' I say, and then immediately wish I hadn't. It's a statistic that I know is very close to her heart.

'No,' she says, 'but we're close. They peak in December and January. That is when my father took his life, of course.'

All those skilful preparations had fooled me into forgetting. They are useful, but they can only take us so far. In winter, you're never more than a few steps from darkness.

★

After a couple of weeks off work, I begin to wonder if I'm unwell after all. Cossetted at home, I've made my own routines that keep me on an even keel: rising at 5am to read; a dose of hot bathwater at 7am; a sedate stroll to the school gates at 8.30. In the day, I read and write, and avoid coffee, and try not to fret about the chaos into which I've thrown my colleagues back at work. Once a fortnight, I call the practice secretary at my GP's surgery, and ask to be signed off again. Nothing has changed, I say. I need more time.

I have given up drinking, just for now. I don't suppose I could ever become permanently teetotal, but at this moment in time I have no appetite for alcohol. I suppose I'm concerned that it will further mutate whatever is in my abdomen. But I'm also suddenly uncomfortably aware of the number of times I reached for it in the last few years as a way of snuffing out the relentless days that left me feeling battered. Anxiety lurked in my body like groundwater, and every now and then it would rain, and the level would rise up into my throat, surging into my sinuses, banking up behind my eyes. The best part of a bottle of wine, or, better still, three large dirty martinis, would quell it for a while. I felt like pouring a drink put a full stop on my day: after this point, I was voluntarily incapable. I couldn't be expected to make any more sensible decisions, or to reply to emails with the necessary delicacy. I was scuppering myself.

Now, my evenings have the consolation of mugs of emerald-green tea made with fresh mint. It's not so bad, but the time seems to stretch, and I'm finding myself in bed by nine, perhaps earlier if I can get away with it. It's a profoundly unsociable way of living, but it gives me those clear-headed early mornings in the inky dark, when I light candles around the house, and relish two straight hours when nobody can make any demands on me. I've got back into the routine of meditating again, now that there's time to do it. Before I sit down, I've developed the habit of opening the back door to sniff the air for a few moments. In the last few weeks, the mornings have smelt fresh and crisp as if the encroaching cold is making everything clean. More recently, it's become gritted with wood smoke, the leftovers of fires the night before. I can smell the changing of the seasons.

All this time is an unfathomable luxury, and I'm struck by the uncomfortable feeling that I'm enjoying it a little too much. Perhaps there is nothing wrong with me at all; perhaps this is all a fantasy that I've concocted in my desperation to leave. I'm only serving my notice period, so perhaps I just don't care anymore. I know that I would certainly be making more of a heroic show of concern for my abandoned post, were I not mentally already out of the door.

In 2016, Oxford Dictionaries named *hygge* their word of the year. The meaning of this Danish term is now well known: it represents cosiness as a kind of mindful practice, a turning towards homely comfort to console us against the harshness of the world outside. I am currently burrowing into a *hyggelig* life, full of candles and tea, judicious quantities of cake, warm jumpers, chunky socks, plenty of time snuggling alone by a lit fire. I wonder if I am perhaps a little too beguiled by this; whether my sense of malaise is actually a lifestyle choice, an urge towards homely perfection to soothe the turmoil that until recently has lurked in my life.

But then I take a short walk to the seafront, and soon the pain comes back. Before it even begins, I notice that I am not quite steady on my feet, listing over slightly sideways in an effort to protect my gut from feeling the full force of my footsteps. Usually, I walk so fast that others beg me to slow down, but today I find myself being overtaken by restless pedestrians, who steer off the narrow Whitstable backstreets and into the roads to get past me.

There is a low brow of cloud over the water. I rest against the sea wall to catch my breath, and watch the yellow-crested waves snap against the shore. At that moment, a text arrives from a colleague, and the sight of her name whirls me into panic. Has somebody spotted me out here? Can I justify taking a walk when everyone else is doubling up to cover my job? I think about how I will have to explain that every step hurt; that I need to build up my strength again.

I open the message. She is only asking, gently, how I am, and whether I can point her to the location of a file. I realise, suddenly, how this season of illness has rearranged my mind into a library of paranoia. I am afraid of being doubted, and I'm afraid of being found out. I am wondering what all those other people, whom I used to see every day, are thinking of me. Are they gossiping, or has some morbid discretion fallen over my name? I'm not sure which is worse. I'm feeling the full force of the guilt of being unable to keep up; of having now fallen so far behind that I can't imagine a way back in. That grinding mix of grief, exhaustion, lost will, lost hope. My only tenable position is to retreat into a dignified silence, but that's not what I want at all. I want to give an account of myself, force everyone else to understand.

Most of all, I want to disappear. I'm almost desperate to find a way to absent myself easily from the situation, like cutting around my outline with a craft knife and cleanly excising myself from the record. But that, I know, would only leave a human-shaped hole. I imagine everybody gazing into the space where I ought to be.

There is a noise overhead, and suddenly the air is full of starlings, all taking flight at once from the surrounding rooftops. A murmuration. There must be a hundred or more of them, silhouetted against the white sky. They disperse over the houses, then join together over the beach as if linked by invisible bonds. Passing me again, they make a loud whisper, the amplified wingbeat of so many birds finding a common purpose, a soft, determined boom.

I have used up all my energy just to see this, and it's worth it. But how could I ever justify that to the outside world? How could I ever admit that I chose the muffled roar of starlings over the noisy demands of the workplace?

I go home, and sleep off the pathetic exertions of my morning.

HOT WATER

S TEPPING INTO THE BLUE LAGOON, I realise that I've been feeling the coming of winter in my bones.

I've spent the day shivering despite a vest and a jumper, a thick coat and a hat with ear-flaps that makes me look like a herdsman from some bleak northern territory. Reykjavik is the kind of penetrating level of cold that feels like nothing initially, but which gradually creeps through your thermal layers and into your very blood. It isn't damp like English cold; just *cold* cold, a kind of purity of coldness that feels absolute.

We have walked through the streets of the capital city and eaten a burger on the harbour. We have sheltered from the cold in the Viking World museum in Keflavík, where we have seen a replica Viking ship and learned some Icelandic sagas. We have eaten mutton stew overlooking the wind-blown Atlantic. We have marvelled at the impossible black volcanic landscape that surrounds us; the way that the tap water smells strongly of sulphur and must be decanted into the fridge for a few hours before it's nearly drinkable. We suspect that we may actually smell of that tap water, but are comforting ourselves with the thought that everyone else must, too, so hopefully no one will notice. We are cold and tired, and slightly anxious about the cost of everything.

But the warm water defrosts us: milky blue and carrying that sulphurous tang, with steam continually rising from its surface into the cold surrounding air. As people wade in, I watch their faces instantly relax, and I'm sure that mine does too. This is like wallowing in calm itself. Perhaps it's the otherworldliness of the opaque water and the black crags of pumice surrounding it; perhaps it's the experience of swimming outside when the sky is grey all around. Perhaps there really is something in the water.

The Blue Lagoon is not a natural phenomenon, but a pool created by the run-off of a geothermal plant. Drilling started in the Svartsengi ('black meadow') lava field in 1976, drawing up steam which is used to generate electricity, and hot water which emerges at over 200°C, packed with minerals and algae. This means that it can't be piped directly into homes because it quickly builds up residues, and so, by a process of heat exchange, it is used to warm fresh water to a useful domestic temperate. The geothermal water is then a waste product, so the original plan was to allow it to run safely off onto the surrounding lava, where it would drain through the naturally occurring cracks and holes. However, within a year, the minerals had started to form a solid layer, which created a pool with distinctive turquoise water created by suspended silica. In 1981, a psoriasis sufferer asked for permission to swim in the pool, and reported that it relieved his symptoms. Gradually, more and more people came to swim there, until a spa was set up in 1992. Its fortunes have matched those of Iceland's burgeoning tourist trade, and a basic day ticket now costs close to £50, with visitors needing to book several weeks in advance.

A monitor in the changing pavilion maps the temperature across the whole lake, which is 37°C in some parts and 39°C in others: about the same as a hot bath. The contrast between the outside air and the water is thrilling. I'm worried that Bert won't join me, but he wades in with great delight, and is soon doggy-paddling beside me as I make my tour of the site. Guests promenade around, clutching cold beers, their faces slathered in white treatment masks made from silica-rich mud. Some, like me, simply float. I notice that a few are carrying their mobile phones in empty plastic glasses to keep them dry, as if they can't be separated from them for even this long. I'm not the only one who has forgotten how to rest.

I spend a while under the thunder of an artificial waterfall, and then haul myself out to sit in the steam grotto, letting the heat penetrate still further. A woman chats to me through the scented fog, and says that the best time of year to come is when there is snow on the ground. I imagine she's right, and immediately regret that I won't be able to see it. Heat is a blunt instrument, but warmth is relative. We feel warmer for knowing that it's freezing outside.

In the changing room later, I experience a different kind of warmth: the nakedness of a dozen women, all unashamed. These aren't the posing bodies you find on the beach, dieted beyond all joy to be bikini-ready, and tanned as an act of disguise. These are northern bodies, slack-bottomed and dimpling, with unruly pubic hair and the scars of hysterectomies, chattering companionably in a language I don't understand. They are a glimpse of life yet to come: a message of survival, passed on through the generations. It's a message I rarely find in my buttoned-up home country, and I think about the times I've suffered silent furies at the treacheries of my own body, imagining them to be unique. We don't know ourselves in context. But there is evidence of wintering here, freely shared like an exchange of precious gifts.

That's what you learn in winter: there is a past, a present and a future. There is a time after the aftermath.

★

In moments of helplessness, I always seem to travel north. I have a kind of boreal wanderlust, an urge towards the top of the world where the ice intrudes. In the cold, I find I can think straight; the air feels clean and uncluttered. I have faith in the practicality of the north, its ability to prepare and endure, the peaks and troughs of its seasons. The warm-weather destinations of the south seem unreal to me, its calendar too unchanging. I love the revolutions that winter brings.

A long time ago – or actually just in August, when everything still seemed possible – we'd planned a trip to Iceland to celebrate my fortieth birthday. When H's appendicitis disrupted my celebrations, we joked in some relief that at least he hadn't booked Iceland on the actual day, or else I might have been tempted to go on my own. But then, with the trip approaching, I decided I shouldn't go at all. I was not well enough. I was not steady enough. I didn't deserve a holiday. Are you even allowed a holiday when you're signed off from work? I was not entirely sure. What on earth would people think if they found out? We've moved a long way from the time when we saw a recuperative break as a legitimate strategy to aid your recovery. I wonder if there's any room left for recovery at all now. We are either off or on.

I had to visit my GP anyway, so I decided to ask for a letter that I could send to my travel insurer to get our money back. It seemed the sensible, responsible thing to do – morally unimpeachable. When she said, 'Can I help you with anything else?' I told her about Iceland, and how, obviously, I wouldn't be able to go. No, she said, I think you should. What difference does it make to be in one country or another, if you're feeling ill anyway? You might as well enjoy these things. You never know what's around the corner.

Receiving a YOLO from a doctor wasn't nearly as comforting as it ought to be. But it's also a glorious endowment of permission from someone who truly knows that you only live once. She probably sits behind that desk every day and watches people learn exactly what lurks around the corner, what howling winters can suddenly descend. I decided to take her advice. A week later, I boarded a plane to Reykjavik.

★

After my swim in the Blue Lagoon, I'm struck down by a fever so violent that it feels as though the waters have drawn it out of me. I put myself to bed and alternate been teeth-chattering shivers and incendiary sweats that leave the bedclothes sodden. My throat might as well be packed with broken glass.

We should really call a doctor, but I don't know how, nor how much it would cost, and in Reykjavik that scares me. Instead, I send H and Bert to see the sights while I lay on the sofa of our Airbnb apartment, watching movies on Netflix and drinking iced water; I carefully alternate paracetamol and ibuprofen in four-hour cycles, and give in to the urge to sleep. I feel as though I have disturbed a dormant kraken by pushing myself too far. But after a day or so, I realise that it's nothing more exotic than tonsillitis. I'm almost pleased with the mundanity of it. It is a simple, known thing. It will pass.

Before long, I'm wondering if I couldn't manage a little trip out in the car. But I'm also being forcibly reminded that this is some kind of a gateway into a new phase in my life. I've been wound so tight with stress that I can no longer see past my own knots, and now, having relaxed ever so slightly, I'm feeling the full force of its impact. I'm run-down. I have skittered over to Iceland in the wake of a bomb blast, and now the aftershock has caught up with me. Life is clearly teaching me some kind of lesson, but I can't decipher it yet. I'm worried that it's about doing less, about staying at home and giving up on adventures for a while. That's not something I want to learn.

Meanwhile, I have the unfamiliar experience of being stuck on the sofa with time to kill. I've brought a pile of books with me to Iceland, but of course I don't want to read them. Instead, I download Philip Pullman's *Northern Lights* on my Kindle, and curl up under the duvet to re-read it. I think I'm craving icy tundra, armoured bears and Dust, hidden cities in the aurora, and the warm embrace of the Gyptians. I often turn to children's books at times like these, when I'm yearning to escape into a world that is beautifully rendered and complex, and yet also soothingly familiar. But as I progress through the story, I realise instead that I'm actually searching for something. I'm haunted by the image of Tony Makarios cleaved from his daemon, and I'm trying to find him in the pages. And after a couple of hours, there he suddenly is: staggering palely towards Lyra, shivering, lost and unable to survive. I have been hunting down a mirror for myself, a representation of how I feel at this moment in time. A severed child, caught between two worlds, not sure if I can believe in any solid future. It's not exactly comforting to find it, but it's certainly satisfying, like a shared moment of outrage or the pleasure of a sad film.

By the end of the holiday, I have recovered sufficiently to board a ship called the *Andrea* and head out to sea in search of whales, if only with the help of a lot of medication. It is now blue skied, crisp and bright outside, and the sea is calm enough to form a perfect mirror in the Old Harbour. Bert, who is already dressed in salopettes and a padded parka, is obliged to wear a lifejacket so enormous that he can barely use his arms. He staggers all over the deck as we head out to sea, and keeps stumbling over like a drunken Michelin man. He simply can't find his sea legs, so soon gets bored, demanding to watch *Ben & Holly's Little Kingdom* on my phone, and making futile attempts to nap on one of the fibreglass benches. Every wave rolls him onto the floor where he gets stranded on his back like an absurd orange beetle, his legs flailing.

All around us, the sea is putting on a spectacle, and he's barely interested. Tiny moon jellyfish dot the surface of the water, and guillemots dive for unseen fish, but glimpses of the cetaceans are intermittent, and he has no sense of their rarity. His books are full of whales, and he sees them – whole – on the TV, howling out their strange cries and making eye contact with the camera. They must seem commonplace to him, and, today, uncooperative. It's one of the great privileges of adulthood to know that there's nothing commonplace in watching a minke whale breaching a few metres from your boat, with its calf following shortly after; nor in watching a pod of dolphins racing in front of the bow, twelve of them jumping out of the water in a synchronised wave. All this life – all this survival – in the deepest cold.

On the way back to shore, I sit on the deck and let the low golden light slant onto my face. This is northern sunbathing: soaking the only part of your body you dare expose to the elements in the most diffuse warmth imaginable, and feeling renewed. I realise that I find my calm in watching the restless patterns the wind makes on the slate-blue Atlantic, far more than I ever could in a tropical paradise that isn't mine. I am native here. What's the point in migrating to a warmer country for a couple of weeks to push winter away? It's just delaying the inevitable. I want to winter in the cold, embrace the changes it brings, acclimatise.

But I know, too, that I have spent most of my life trying to push winter away, having rarely had to truly feel its bite. Growing up in south-east England, where snow is a rarity and the darkness can always be repelled with a lightbulb, I have never had to prepare for winter. I have never had to endure months of brutal cold, or being cut off. In Iceland – where roads will soon close after the first snowfalls, and life has to cling tenaciously to the windswept lava – I have learned something about keeping warm. Here, on the deck of the *Andrea* in the outer reaches of the Atlantic, and approaching a personal winter, I'm suddenly certain that the cold has healing powers that I don't yet come close to understanding. After all, you apply ice to a joint after an awkward fall. Why not do the same to a life?

On our final day, we drive across country to see the 'golden triangle': the Gullfoss waterfall, all crowds, thunder and refracted rainbows; Strokkur the geyser, which bulges and grumbles and then explodes in a magnificent column of boiling water; and the meeting of the North American and Eurasian tectonic plates in Þingvellir National Park. Driving back through the treeless countryside, I think I have spotted the sea on the far horizon, and believe that we've driven all the way across the island. But, on consulting our map, I realise that it is a glacier, a huge field of permanent ice that glimmers like water. I had no idea that it was there. I had no idea that it was even possible.

I realise that I am not nearly done with this bizarre, otherworldly country, so full of ice and heat, so teeming with mythology. We agree that we will return in easier times.

★

When I was talking to Hanne Mällinen-Scott, I noticed that she returned again and again to the sauna, and the way that it helps her to cope with the cold. On returning home from Iceland, I realised that this was a little of what I'd experienced in the Blue Lagoon: the warming of the body, but also the easing of the mind.

The sauna has an almost spiritual significance in the Finnish psyche, acting as a place of relaxation and retreat, particularly in those winter months. Most houses have their own sauna, and in blocks of flats there will be a communal one in which you have an allocated time-slot each week. Not having access to a sauna is unthinkable. It's seen as an essential, like a bathroom or kitchen.

'It's a calm time,' Hanne said, 'a family time. You experience a clearing of the mind in sauna.' Hanne's English is flawless, but I noticed that she used this phrase again and again: *in sauna*, rather than *in the sauna*. She's not talking about a building, a little pine shed with burning coals in the corner; she's talking about a state of being.

'All the decisions are made there,' she said. 'My mother was born in sauna.' She saw me looking horrified: the idea of labouring in such a hot environment makes me nauseous. 'Everyone was! It was the cleanest place in those times, and all your hot water would be in there anyway. You were taken in there to be washed when you died, too.' Until very recently, the sauna hosted the entire lifecycle. The whole run, from birth to death, is still symbolically there, brought close by the winter.

'What do you do after your sauna?' I asked.

'You run into a lake if you can,' she said, 'or roll naked in the snow.'

I stared at her for a few moments. 'Are you joking?' I said.

'No!' she said. 'It's lovely. If it's summer, you light a fire and all sit around cooking sausages on sticks. But in winter it's more of an occasion because you need the heat. We had a special room where we could all sit together on our towels and have a drink. You need it because you feel so isolated.'

The cold lakes and piles of snow will not be forthcoming, but I nevertheless vow that I will devote half an hour each week to sitting in the sauna at my local gym, after a gentle swim. I hope that it will give me a little of that northern clarity; a little of that vital contrast against the coldness of life. In fact, I imagine myself sitting contentedly in the hot, pine twilight of the sauna, drinking in mystic wisdom, and improving my pores no end.

I intimate as much to H, who says, 'You hate saunas. They make you too hot.'

'Yes,' I reply, 'but I've realised that I just have to lower my resistance to being hot, and I'll start enjoying it. I have to stop seeing hot as a bad thing.'

A couple of years ago, I shared a sauna with a friend who poured water on the coals so enthusiastically that I had to scamper out of the cabin in fear that I'd be scalded. I was sure that he would follow me straight out and admit his mistake, but he only emerged ten minutes later, lobster pink and with a dreamy smile on his face. I have decided that this will become a learning point: I need not have feared the heat. I must instead learn to surrender to it.

I pay my membership fee, swim a chlorinated and increasingly bored twenty lengths, and then retire to the steam room to acclimatise. I am comfortable here, in the dense, warm fog, feeling my skin grow damp and supple, letting my lungs expand and feel clean. This has always seemed to me to be the more appealing room of the two: the sauna is sparse and dry, but the steam room is warm and accommodating. And yet hard-core users of the global hammam seem to admire the sauna over all else, as the mother of all hot rooms. Is it just because the sauna is an acquired taste, harder to love and so more revered; or is it simply because it's a more basic format, just a wooden shed, hot coals and a splash of water? The sauna seems natural where the steam room is municipal, with its moulded seats and thermostatically controlled fug. Loving the steam room is akin to loving a newly built mall over a quaint market town. It's tacky. I need to get over it.

So I unpeel myself from the hot plastic, unhook my towel from the peg, and pad into the sauna, which is, thankfully, empty, and looks as though it may have been unused for some time. The room is pleasantly warm, rather than searingly hot; the heater ticks away in the corner.

I lay out my towel and perch on the bottom bench, which, I am assured, is the coolest spot in the room. I breathe in the arid air and cough. I decide that this is probably a good thing. I am expectorating! This, surely, will be the magic of the sauna. I lean back and then regret it, suspecting that my back is now branded with bench stripes.

It does smell good in here: woody and faintly resinous. My skin prickles and feels as though it may be puckering; the roots of my hair tingle. The temperature is certainly rising. I try to find the sauna state of mind, spacious and peaceful, free of the immediate concerns of life outside the door. Instead, I feel mainly thirsty. I breathe. It won't be long before I can get a drink. For now, I am 'in sauna'. I am doing what I did in Iceland: seeking out the elemental force of heat, and finding a way to ride over the bumps of human life. This is not an indulgence. This is a stern, solid maintenance mode, a hardy response to the vagaries of existence. I am being practical.

I am also done. Done, as in cooked through. You could put a skewer in me and find my juices running clear. That is fine. Because of my time in the sauna, I am now wise and clear-headed, so I know that it is not worth pushing myself past all comfort, and that I can build up my resistance over time. I get up, wrap my towel around my shoulders, and slope off into the showers.

It is at this moment – while the warm water is pounding my scalp and my lungs are relishing the return to cool air – that I begin to feel a little dizzy. I take a few deep breaths, but my heart is pounding, and my vision is flashing between entirely normal, and a strange dark green with golden edges. I'm all right, though; I am, after all, sufficiently compos mentis to be able to analyse the situation. I possibly just need some water. Now I come to think of it, my mouth is incredibly dry.

I turn off the shower and go back to my cubicle to sit down for a while. While I'm doing that, I manage to pull on my knickers, because the thought has now overtaken me that I am naked under a towel, and feeling rather faint, and in a locked cubicle, and that I really ought to remove myself from that situation. I have just managed to hook on my bra when I realise that I might be sick. Or that I might black out entirely. The best thing, surely, is to lie down on the floor, on my side, so that no harm can come to me if anything happens.

I lie there for quite some time, my face pressed against the cold, verruca-damp tiles, watching the feet of a handful of women walking to and fro, moisturising their shins and pulling on socks. I am absolutely fine, overall, if a little concerned that the anti-slip texture of the flooring is now imprinted on my cheek. I once got heatstroke at a music festival and incorrectly told everyone in the medical tent that I was with my three brothers, who were identical triplets, but that I couldn't remember their names. My (lone, actual) brother heard this announcement over the tannoy, and somehow realised that it must be me. I am certainly not in that sort of state now. I am actually feeling almost astonishingly lucid, if a little bit attached to the floor. And incredibly thirsty.

I try to lift my head, but the world swims again, so I decide that I can maybe gain some discreet assistance from the woman in the cubicle next door, who has been clanking around with bags and bottles for quite some time.

'Excuse me,' I whisper, and then say it louder: 'Excuse me?' I tap on the partition between us.

'Yes?' comes a startled voice.

'I'm sorry to trouble you, but I'm feeling a little faint. I wonder if you could possibly get me a glass of water?'

A pause.

'Er, is it absolutely necessary? Only, I'm in the middle of getting dressed.'

'Yes,' I croak. 'I can't seem to get up off the floor.'

The woman falls silent, and it looks for all the world as though she's thought better of conversing with me, and has decided to just get on with her day.

In time, she leaves the cubicle, and I hear the door to the changing room shut too. Everybody has gone.

And then, suddenly, everybody has not gone. The door swings open, and in rushes a woman shouting, 'I'm looking for the lady who's fainted!'

Oh God, I think. She asks if I can open my cubicle, and I can. I begin to explain that all I really need is a glass of water, but at that moment I realise that she is just the advance party. In rushes what seems to be the entire staff, half of them male and two of them carrying defibrillators. They all form an expectant semicircle around me, looking concerned and also overwhelmingly excited by the prospect of putting their first aid training to use. My only thought is that my effort to put on my underwear before I took up residency on the floor now seems like an act of heroism.

'Get them out of here!' I whisper to the first woman, who is now my ally because she is the only other person in the room who also dwells on the northern face of forty. 'I am in my *underwear*,' I add, for emphasis.

Thankfully, she agrees. She picks up my towel and drapes it over me, and tells the assembled crowd that I am conscious, and that they can therefore safely disperse.

'Sorry,' she says, 'we put an announcement out over the radio for first aiders, and they all came.'

'I only need a glass of water,' I say. 'Really.'

Finally, my water is forthcoming. I sit up to drink it, and begin to feel better. To fast-forward the rest, I then sit in the massage suite for an hour, sipping sugary tea and being talked into taking a taxi, because, really, it isn't safe to drive in my state. That costs me twenty-five quid, plus the three months' notice on my gym membership, because I am not setting foot in that place ever again.

Perhaps, then, it's a mistake to adopt the practices of the North wholesale. Perhaps it takes a lifetime to acclimatise. Perhaps it just isn't yet time.

Perhaps I need to feel the true cold before I can warm up again.

GHOST STORIES

HALLOWEEN IS THE BORDER-CROSSING into winter. Technically, November is an autumn month too, with leaves still clinging to the trees. But psychologically, a line is crossed here. The following day, when the pumpkins begin to moulder, my thoughts turn to Christmas, and getting in firewood, and wearing tights under my jeans on Bonfire Night.

Halloween was barely anything when I was a child, but now, like Christmas, there's a distinct run-up to the day itself, and we return from Iceland to find it in full swing. Along my street, people have stuck cut-outs of ghosts and bats in their windows, and paperchains of interlinked pumpkins festoon doorways. In the window of the hardware shop in town, someone has draped a mannequin in a black cloak, and topped it with a hor-rific mask that has greenish skin, straining eyeballs and a mouth fixed in a scream. As a child, I remember a pair of trick-or-treaters knocking on my grandparents' door, and I had to hide behind my nanna's skirt because I'd never seen such a terrible thing before. But Bert seems to breeze through the ghoulish imagery; in fact, he craves it, grumbling that we have yet again failed to decorate the house with cotton-wool cobwebs and plastic gravestones.

'We don't do Halloween,' I tell him, as we pass yet another shop window full of skeletal remains and severed fingers. 'It's not our tradition.'

'But why?' he says, and I don't have a ready answer for that. Because it seems excessive to me: tacky, unnecessarily costly and full of enervating new customs that do not happen by common consent? Because it's new? Because Halloween night always feels like it's just about to veer into chaos, and I'm uneasy every time I pass a group of teenagers? Last year, we woke up on 1 November to find that our front door had been pelted with eggs, their shattered shells embedded in the paintwork. Despite having waited meekly by the door all evening to hand out sweets to anyone who knocked, I had somehow been targeted for a nasty trick. I told myself that it was random, while secretly imagining that they'd sniffed out my fear.

Halloween is an overturning of the natural order, though, and has its lineage in old traditions of reversing the roles, letting the poor become rulers, and bringing the rich low. There has long been a feverish link between monsters and mockery, and those without power have often been given licence to play at the edges of civility in order to quell more dangerous lurches towards riot and rebellion. At Halloween, the next generation (who, after all, seem unlikely to be able to afford their own version of my pitted front door) get to express their wound-up potential for making trouble, and so offer us a comforting vision of the restraint they show for the rest of the year. For Bert, who is a decade away from all-out insurgency, Halloween is the festival that gives him access to the encroaching winter nights, letting him dress up and go brazenly out into the dark evening, knocking on unfamiliar doors. Guy Fawkes Night interests him, but not enough. He wants the camp pantomime of Halloween, the last outpost of summer before his playtime gets seriously restricted by the dark.

'Next year,' I find myself telling him, 'we'll decorate. I promise.'

★

We've come a long way since Halloween was merely the night before Hallowmas, the day the Christian faithful remembered the sacrifices of their saints. According to Steve Roud in *The English Year*, the vigils held on the eve of All Saints' Day had become more like parties by the nineteenth century, with apple bobbing and other games. This was also the time for simple acts of divination, many of which predicted the ways of love. Apples were peeled in one long, unbroken strip, which was tossed over your shoulder to reveal the initial of your beloved; hazelnuts were named after yourself and the person you desired, and then roasted at the side of the fire. If the nuts jumped away from the heat, it was taken as a bad sign for your future marital harmony. More eerily, a woman could brush her hair in front of a mirror at midnight and hope to glimpse her future husband over her shoulder.

In Halloween, we see echoes of the Gaelic pagan festival of Samhain, which marked the arrival of the 'dark half' of the year. It was celebrated with bonfires and burning torches, the scattering of ashes and attempts to see the future through dreams or the flight of crows. Most importantly, Samhain was considered to be a moment when the veil between this world and the otherworld was at its thinnest. Old gods had to be placated with gifts and sacrifice, and the trickery of fairies was an even greater risk than usual. This was a liminal moment in the calendar: a time between two worlds, and between two phases of the year, when worshippers were just about to cross a boundary but hadn't yet done so.

Samhain was a way of marking that ambiguous moment when you didn't know who you were about to become, or what the future would hold. It was a celebration of limbo.

Our contemporary celebrations forget the dead altogether, or at least remove them from any association with grief and loss. They offer no comfort to those who mourn. We are, after all, a society that has done all it can to erase death, to pursue youth to the bitter end, and to sideline the elderly and infirm. For most of us, the old tradition of laying-out our own dead is long forgotten; the idea that we might be intimate with death is now some kind of a gothic joke. Today's Halloween only reflects what we secretly think: that death is a surrender to a decay that makes us monsters.

But winter is a time when death comes closest: when the cold feels as though it might yet snatch us away, despite our modern comforts. We still perceive the presence of those we've lost in the silence of those long evenings, and in the depths of darkness that they bring. This is the season of ghosts. Their pale forms are invisible in bright sunlight. Winter makes them clear again.

★

When Halloween night finally arrives, I give in. Bert goes out trick-or-treating with a friend, and when they both come back I serve them a special tea of pumpkin soup and dead man's fingers (hot dogs with fried onion worms), and a chocolate cake that oozes green icing. They bob apples in the back garden and paint their faces as skeletons, with white cheeks and black eye sockets. He goes off to bed that night contented, if a little wild with the excitement and the sugar. He's already planning a costume for next year. I feel as though I have sanctioned an act of rebellion on a school night, and that pleases me.

That night, I read a few pages of my childhood favourite, Lucy M. Boston's *The Children of Green Knowe*. Amid all the ghoulish cacophony, I need a true ghost story: quiet and crisply written, eerie rather than horrific, and finding its meaning in liminality. Like so many mid-century children's novels, it opens at the beginning of the Christmas holidays, with young Tolly sitting on a train, returning from boarding school to his ancestral home. His parents are in Burma, so he'll be staying with his great-grandmother, Linnet Oldknow, a woman of great kindness and subtle witchery. The house initially strikes Tolly as a lonely place, but soon he realises that there are children there to play with, if only sometimes: the ghosts of past Tollys and Oldknows.

Green Knowe seems to be an eternal present, where many times merge into one; a Celtic 'thin place' where ghosts can easily seep through to the present day. Soon, Tolly is battling ancient evils with the other children, but also learning the songs they loved and playing with their toys. There are objects in the house – a little ebony mouse, a pair of china dogs – that represent a collective pooling of imagination between the many generations of children who have lived in Green Knowe: 'Did the mouse squeak under your pillow and the dogs bark?' asks Mrs Oldknow when Tolly wakes the first morning.

But reading *The Children of Green Knowe* tonight, I am struck most of all by a passage towards the end of the book, which was probably invisible to my childish eyes. On Christmas Eve, Tolly and his great-grandmother dress the tree together, and then hear the sound of a cradle rocking coming from upstairs. Soon it is accompanied by a woman's voice singing:

Lully Lulla, Thou little tiny child
By by, Lully Lullay.
O sisters too, how may we do
For to preserve this day
This poor youngling
For whom we sing
By by, Lully Lullay.

Tolly asks who is singing, and then why his granny is crying. The voice, she says, is so old that she hardly knows whose it is: 'It is lovely, only it is such a long time ago. I don't know why that should be sad, but it sometimes seems so.' Not really understanding what she means, Tolly joins in with the song, 'while, four hundred years ago, a baby went to sleep'. How is it that we can code so carefully the weight of loss, grief, time and continuity into our children's books, but forget them so thoroughly ourselves?

Ghosts may be a part of the terror of Halloween, but our love of ghost stories betrays a far more fragile desire: that we do not fade so easily from this life. We spend a lot of time talking about leaving a legacy in this world, grand or small, financial or reputational, so that we won't be forgotten. But ghost stories show us a different concern, hidden under our bluster: we hope that the dead won't forget us. We hope that we, the living, will not lose the meanings that seem to evaporate when our loved ones die.

My own grandmother died, quite unexpectedly, when I was seventeen. I realise that it sounds absurd to say that about somebody who blew out the candles on her eightieth birthday cake in a hospital bed, but it was my first encounter with death, and it was unexpected to me. In my naive way, I had expected her to get better and come home.

She and I shared an interest in ghost stories, although I think, in reality, that my true passion only really began after she died. Rationalist though I was, I realised that the matter of ghosts was far from settled for me until that point; I felt certain that if anyone could come back on a spectral visit, it would be her. It's hard to express what a bitter disappointment I felt that she didn't manage to appear at my bedside in the middle of the night, radiating comfort. But then, that's what grief is: a yearning for that one last moment of contact that would settle everything. I felt it most keenly for the first year, but it's never gone away. There are just some things that I would say, now, that I didn't think to say when I was seventeen. There are just some things I know now, that I did not know back then.

Halloween is no longer a time for remembrance, but it still reveals our need to enter liminal spaces: those moments when we're standing on the breach of fear and delight, and those times when we wish that the veil between the living and the dead would lift for a while. But most of all, it hints at the winter to come, opening the door to the dark season, and reminding us of the darknesses that lurk in all our futures. We adults should learn to mark it, I think, but not necessarily with the commercialised disorder of our current Halloween. Perhaps we should draw on the rituals of Samhain: light bonfires, placate old gods, and do our best to divine the future. Somewhere, somehow, we will be shown the way to the next world.

NOVEMBER

METAMORPHOSIS

THERE IS A CHANGE IN the air. Early morning, when I open the back door, it billows into the kitchen, crisp, cold and fresh as mint. It makes white clouds of my breath. Winter has decorated ordinary life. Some days, everything sparkles, glamorising the lids of bins and the tarmac patchwork of the pavements. Frost etches mysterious patterns on the roof of our car, and the puddles that collect in the gutter are crisp with ice.

My cats have taken on their winter coats. Lulu, our black and white moggy, is Marmite brown in the summer, but goes boot-polish black when the cold comes; Heidi, our tortoiseshell, loses her warm-weather blondes and becomes plush and velvety, her gingery tones deepening to red. They are suddenly present in the house, having avoided us all summer when the warm nights invite adventure. Just like us, they are craving comfy cushions and the occasional fire.

I'm changing too. Now that they're wrapped in socks all day, my feet turn from their summer brown to winter white, and my sunshine freckles fade away. My shins and knees are drying out; my face drinks in moisturiser every morning. Deprived of sun, my hair darkens, and the skin frays around my nails. Mine is a drab winter coat, usually lifted by bright red cheeks, the legacy of coastal winds. But then, winter is no time to put on a display. I love the separation it brings, the way that people are scarce even during the daylight hours, when you can drink in the dilute light of the low sun, your shadow stretching long at your feet.

As the year progresses, I'm growing used to being in pain. After a few weeks of antibiotics, my head is feeling clearer again, and I'm obediently taking my painkillers to stave off the worst of it. I'm beginning to venture outside again, just in short bursts. This is the season when I start to believe that the beach is all mine, miles of windswept solitude that I can march along without encountering another soul. Nobody else seems to enjoy the cold or the bluster as I do. Winter is the best season for walking, as long as you can withstand a little earache and are immune to mud. On the coldest days, even that freezes solid, and the ground crunches underfoot, firm and satisfying. A good frost will pick out every blade of grass, the crenellated edge of every leaf. The cold renders everything exquisite.

I walk along the River Stour at Sandwich, heading out across the flats and towards the sea at Pegwell Bay. The reeds have dried to a rustling beige, and the bare trees reveal a bright green woodpecker, flitting between branches. I notice that the black-headed gulls have already put on their winter plumage. The juveniles, entering their first winter, have simply turned their brown feathers to grey. The breeding adults look nearly completely white as they glide overhead, the dark feathers on their faces having retreated to leave just a charcoal smudge behind each eye, like a comic ear. They are still every bit as agile, though, and every bit as hungry.

The tide is higher than usual, and the marsh is transformed into a low, silvery sea. This has displaced the curlews into the undergrowth around the path; as I walk along, they scatter at my feet, fluting bad temperedly. There are pheasants, too, and a peregrine being mobbed by crows. Amid the transformation of winter – the unwelcome change – is an abundance of life.

★

'There was a point,' says Shelly Goldsmith, 'when my mother had to peel a grape, put it in my mouth, and move my jaw to make me chew. It was the only way I could eat.'

I'm sitting in Shelly's office, overlooking the River Medway, which is grey and indistinct today.

'Do you mind talking about it?' I say. 'I mean, are you sure?'

'Of course,' she says, and I think she means it. Now that I'm here, clutching the cup of camomile tea she's made me, the intimacy of my request has finally dawned on me. Illness is usually a private affair, and this is perhaps even truer of a sudden, catastrophic illness like Shelly's, which tears you unexpectedly from the very weave of life.

But I'm looking for something, and hers was the story that instantly came to mind when I thought about that liminal state: the girl who, at seventeen, fell into a coma, and took a year to recover. The reason I believe her when she says she doesn't mind is that it's clear that this experience turned her into something extraordinary. I want to know how she got from there to here. I want to understand the depths of that winter, and how you claw yourself back from it.

I've known Shelly for a long while, and she's one of those rare people who manage to be warm and kind, and pin-sharp clever at the same time. An award-winning textile artist, her work has been exhibited in major galleries and museums across the world. She works with garments, or re-appropriates old ones: children's dresses or vintage nighties that are then printed and stitched, laser-etched and unpicked, simultaneously delicate and fierce. They ring with the fragility of life and the vulnerability of children, the push-and-pull between mothers and daughters, the tension between how we begin, and what we become. Within them, I can always detect the whisper of hospital sheets and the looming threat of the institution.

'I thought I had the flu,' she says. She had just started an art foundation year, and her parents were on holiday in America, so one of her lecturers drove her home. She ended up being put to bed at her neighbours' house because her sister needed to go out to work and didn't think she should be left alone. A doctor was called, but didn't think it was anything particularly serious, so she tried to sleep it off.

The last thing Shelly remembers of that night is waking up and feeling so sick and frightened that she called out, 'Help me, I'm dying!' She reached for the door handle, and had only just touched it when everything went black.

Her hosts came in and found that she had crawled to the other side of the room and wedged herself under the dressing table. They called an ambulance, and Shelly had to be strapped down into the stretcher because she was convulsing so badly. That's when she fell into a coma. Her parents rushed back from America to find their daughter unconscious in a hospital bed, with a fifty–fifty chance of staying alive.

But Shelly remembers none of this, because she was having the most extraordinary dream. She reached out for the door handle and then heard singing. She realised that she was falling through darkness, but the singing, somehow, caught her and carried her up again, over the top of a cliff, across some grass and into a caravan. There, she found a pair of eyes floating in the space, and they were the source of the song. She knew instinctively that they were her dead aunt's, and that they had saved her.

She opened her eyes, and no time had passed at all, but there she was, in the isolation ward of Rush Green Hospital in Romford, surrounded by her parents and her sister, three days later. The flu turned out to be bacterial meningitis.

It seems to me to be the most shattering of experiences, to fall so quickly from good health to near-death; it must have changed everything. But Shelly folds her hands in her lap. 'And after that,' she says, 'it took me a year to recover. I had to start university all over again, in a different town.'

That's it. The End.

'Wait,' I say. 'Tell me about your time in hospital. How long were you there?'

'Oh,' she says breezily, 'a month and a half, I suppose.'

'How did you feel?'

She shrugs. 'It was hard to move at first. I couldn't do anything for myself. My mother had to be there all the time to look after me.'

'And?' I say.

'And there were loads of drugs to take. Everyone came in all masked up, because I was so contagious. The ward was just a little row of beds in the middle of a field. Or that's how I remember it, anyway. I'm probably completely wrong. It was a long time ago.'

'So you had physio to get you back on your feet again?'

'No, I just gradually got better.'

'And once you got home?'

'I can't remember. I watched TV, I suppose. I'd missed everything at college, so I couldn't go back to class. I didn't like the thought of it, anyway – going back to the same place. So I had to wait the rest of the year to start all over again.'

I think I'm seeking some heroic story of triumph over illness, some kind of deliberate struggle and fight. A path through, that she can pass on; a methodology. But it's not there. It's not the story. It's of no interest to Shelly: a blank time, when very little happened. She waited it out. That's all she could do. She didn't even assimilate what happened; she just carried on.

'I didn't witness it,' she says. 'I didn't have to stand there looking at my daughter in a coma.' It took years for her to realise how close she had been to death, and to gain a sense of how thoroughly she'd teetered on the edge of that cliff. Even so, after her year of waiting was up, she went back to university with a renewed sense of focus and determination. At eighteen years old, she already knew what it was possible to lose.

I'm almost disappointed. It's an extraordinary story, but there's nothing to learn from it. You wait it out. And once things are better, you forget the quality of 'it' altogether. That part of you gets cast aside, happily forgotten. Life begins to happen again, and that makes for more compelling memories. I was hoping to look into the eye of the storm, but I'm only left with its aftermath.

'That part of me is a bit of a ghost, to be honest,' says Shelly. 'Look, I know you want to talk about the coma, but when you described wintering to me, something else came to mind. I thought about my parents leaving England instead. That's when I think I actually wintered.'

So she begins to tell me another story: when she was twenty-five, her parents decided to move to America, following her sister who had emigrated a couple of years before. The decision seemed to come from nowhere. That was it: a sudden severance from the support network she'd had all her life. Once they were gone, it was nearly impossible to speak to them, because she couldn't afford the transatlantic phone calls, and the time zones made it difficult. They would all need to arrange to be near a phone at the same time, and how did you do that in the first place? Her parents seemed preoccupied with their new lives, anyway. She felt as though she had disappeared from view.

This was a bereavement as profound as anything brought about by death, made all the more painful because to her mind her parents had chosen to leave. Yet Shelly's grief was invisible to everyone around her. Her friends just didn't think it was a big deal: nobody had actually died, after all. They didn't understand the cliff face between someone literally helping you to chew your food so you can stay alive, and then them leaving you behind. But Shelly felt unmoored, precarious. She was living with a boyfriend at the time, and their relationship was breaking down. There was no home to run back to, and no money to tide her over while she found somewhere else to live. When they finally split, she was left homeless, sleeping on sofas and nursing a sense of sadness that she felt she wasn't supposed to have.

And there it is: that howling experience of the cold and the dark that becomes a crucible; that senses of falling through the crack between two worlds. She's right: this is a wintering. That void – that state of limbo – led her somewhere. From the depths of her unhappiness, she was drawn to start working on a new creative project, using unwanted children's clothes donated from an orphanage. She didn't make the connection to her own life at first. But after a while, she began to feel a commonality with the former owners of all those tiny dresses. She realised that she had started to talk about her family as though they were gone, and that she felt orphaned herself; she had found a way to mark out her common ground with other displaced children. It was a breakthrough moment for her, an artwork that established her reputation. And it came from the deepest of winters: from having come back from the dead, only to be left alone.

There's another thing about orphans, too: they have to look after themselves and take control of their own destinies, because no one else will give them a leg-up. It became a framework for the way Shelly saw the world, making her believe in her own resourcefulness: 'I think I've got a great capacity to bounce back. I'm stubborn,' she says. But it also made her more compassionate and humane. 'You realise that no one is what they look like on the surface.' Everybody has their dose of suffering; it's just more hidden in some than in others.

I get the sense that the time she spent suspended in that dream state, being sung into safety, has echoed through the rest of her life. It has made her more conscious of achieving what she can in case the next disaster strikes, but at the same time it has removed her fear of death. She tells me that she flew out to the US this summer to help her sister switch off her comatose husband's life support. It was a rite of passage, a moment when she realised she was able to be a guide, because she knew how it felt to die. 'He'd have known nothing about it,' she says. 'No pain, no fear. He'll only have remembered going into hospital and ordering dinner.' The rest, she is certain, would have been one kind of bliss or another, not exactly like her dream, but something similar.

As I'm packing up my things and thanking Shelly for her time, she starts to tell me about her plans for the coming year. She hopes to travel to Japan to take part in the annual Needle Mass, a festival in which seamstresses give thanks for the tools of their trade. They hold ceremonies in which they bring their broken needles into temples, and lay them reverently to rest by embedding them in slabs of tofu. Shelly's creative life has hinged on setting millions of tiny stitches, and she loves the idea of taking part.

'I think about this a lot,' she says. 'The needle breaks the fabric in order to repair it. You can't have one without the other.'

★

Transformation is the business of winter. In Gaelic mythology, the hag deity known as the Cailleach takes human form at Samhain to rule the winter months, bringing in winds and wild weather. Her very steps change the land: the mountains of Scotland were formed when she dropped rocks from her basket, and she carries a hammer for forming valleys. A touch of her staff is enough to freeze the ground. But the Cailleach is thought to be the mother of the gods, the gruff, cold originator of all things. Her reign only lasts until Beltane, at the beginning of May, when Brighde takes over, and the Cailleach turns to stone. In some versions of the mythology, the Cailleach and Brighde are two faces of the same goddess: youth and vitality for summer, age and wisdom for winter.

As we so often find in ancient folklore, the Cailleach offers us a cyclical metaphor for life, one in which the energies of spring can arrive again and again, nurtured by the deep retreat of winter. We are no longer accustomed to thinking in this way. We are instead in the habit of imagining our lives to be linear; a long march from birth to death in which we mass our powers, only to surrender them again, all the while slowly losing our youthful beauty. This is a brutal untruth. Life meanders like a path through the woods. We have seasons when we flourish, and seasons when the leaves fall from us, revealing our bare bones. Given time, they grow again.

The dropping of leaves by deciduous trees is called 'abscission'. It occurs on the cusp of autumn and winter, as part of a long cycle of growth, maturity and renewal. In spring and summer, leaf cells are full of chlorophyll, a bright green substance that absorbs sunlight to fuel the process that converts carbon dioxide and water into the starch and sugar that allow the tree to grow. But at the end of the summer, as the days grow shorter and the temperature falls, deciduous trees stop making food. In the absence of sunlight, it would be too costly to maintain the machinery of growth. The chlorophyll begins to break down, revealing other colours that were always present in the leaf, but which were masked by the abundance of green pigment: oranges and yellows, derived from carotene and xanthophyll. At the same time, other chemical changes take place to create red anthocyanin pigments. The exact mix is different for each tree, sometimes producing bright yellows, oranges and browns, and sometimes displaying as reds or purples. The trees put on their autumn display.

But while this is happening, a layer of cells is weakening between the stem and the branch: this is called the abscission zone. Gradually it severs the leaf from access to water, and the leaf dries and browns, and then in most cases falls off, either under its own weight, or encouraged by wintery rains and winds.

Within a few hours, the tree will have released substances that heal the scar that the leaf has left, protecting itself from the evaporation of water, infection or the invasion of parasites.

But even as the leaves are falling, the buds of next year's crop are already in place, waiting to erupt again in spring. Most trees produce their buds in high summer, and the autumn leaf fall reveals them, neat and expectant, protected from the cold by thick scales. We rarely notice them because we think we're seeing the skeleton of the tree, a dead thing until the sun returns. But look closely, and every single tree is in bud, from the sharp talons of the beech to the hoof-like black buds of the ash. Many trees also display catkins in the winter, like the acid green lambs' tails of the hazel and the furry grey nubs of the willow. These employ the wind or insects to spread pollen, ready for the new year.

The tree is waiting. It has everything ready. Its fallen leaves are mulching the forest floor, and its roots are drawing up the extra winter moisture, providing a firm anchor against seasonal storms. Its ripe cones and nuts are providing essential food in this scarce time for mice and squirrels, and its bark is hosting hibernating insects and providing a source of nourishment for hungry deer. It is far from dead. It is, in fact, the life and soul of the wood. It's just getting on with it quietly. It will not burst into life in the spring. It will just put on a new coat and face the world again.

The starkness of winter can reveal colours that we would otherwise miss. I once watched a fox cross a frosty field, her coat shining against the gloom. Walking in the bare winter woodland, I am also surrounded by astonishing foxy reds: the burnish of bracken, its dry fronds twisted to lacework; the crimson leaves left on brambles; the last remaining berries on honeysuckle; and orangey clusters of rosehips. The iconic holly, its boughs so thoroughly raided each Christmas. There is also the bright yellow of gorse on heathland, glowing on until spring comes, the stately evergreens, and the tangle of green leaves that remain unnoticed on the ground. Life goes on, abundantly, in winter, and this is where changes are made that usher us into future glories.

★

A hospital is a particular kind of winter. Jenny Diski captures it well in *Skating to Antarctica*: the layers of sterile white that offer both discipline and comfort, often at the same time; the sense of personal obliteration. It's a temple to a certain kind of faith, the residual trust that there is a higher authority that knows the answers, and which can save us. I imagine Shelly Goldsmith in her ward, and I can't help but bring to mind the Ladybird book I had as a child, full of nurses in immaculate starched dresses and cheerful patients in striped pyjamas, tucked safely under red blankets. The floors polished until they look like water in miles of corridor; the lingering smell of disinfectant. All of these things shepherd us into another state of being, where we are compliant, passive, helpless – and willingly so. We fall easily into a hierarchy that we would resist in any other situation. We will undergo whatever transformations the institution requires of us. We will not make a fuss. We will be good. We will do as we're told.

I've had all I can stomach in recent weeks. In the mission to find the source of my abdominal pain, I've endured tests and procedures that involve fasting and violent doses of laxatives, painful and undignified investigations. There have been insinuations that I ought to prepare for the worst. I don't know what frightens me more: the possibility of a life-threatening diagnosis, or coming away with nothing other than shame at my own ability to malinger.

Eventually, I find myself in a room with a weary-looking nurse who tells me that I have the gut of a particularly self-neglectful seventy year old. I hold within me a maze of spasms and inflammations, a wonderland of malabsorption. It is a strange diagnosis to process: nothing like as bad as I'd feared, but life-changing, nonetheless. It will not simply go away. It will flare and recur, demand careful management and eternal vigilance. I find myself protesting about how carefully I eat, how I cook from scratch and drink litres of water. I don't mention the night-time martinis, and the canteen lunches wolfed down during improvised meetings or in the car home. I am a reformed character now. I want to be allowed to bask in the glory of my recovery from the brink, rather than to still be teetering on the edge of it, no matter what I do.

I am sent to a dietician, who provides me with a few simple new rules for eating, to which I react with bad grace. I am given instructions for a low-fibre diet, just for a week, and I somehow manage to make it sound as though I have never heard of white carbs, and can't get by without a daily infusion of lentils and kale. 'It's only for a few days,' says the dietician, mystified. 'It's not forever.'

And it isn't. It's actually surprisingly speedy, and ever so slightly luxurious. I spend three days eating egg fried rice and spaghetti with butter, white toast and Marmite and bacon sandwiches. It's the most counter-intuitive diet I've ever followed, and it fills me with guilt, and also makes me feel better than I have in months. The effect is almost instant: the bizarre sensation that I can straighten up again, that I can actually digest what I eat, that my energy has returned.

Quicker than I ever hoped, I land at the other side of my illness: slightly battle-scarred, slightly hungrier, and an awful lot wiser. I have flaws. I live with restrictions. I have to change. But those sacrifices now seem easy to make, knowing what they will give me. I feel as though I, too, have shed some leaves: those last shreds of belief in my youthful robustness, when I could do anything, endure anything, and believe I could bounce back. Winter is asking me to be more careful with my energies, and to rest a while until spring.

SLUMBER

I MAY LOVE THE GREAT outdoors in winter, but even I draw the line at sunset. When November comes, I have no desire to leave the house after dark. My instinct is to hibernate the evenings aways. I hate those strange walks along the high street, lit only by street lamps and the glow of shop windows, the cold seeping up your coat sleeves. I don't like the way that four o'clock in the afternoon can feel so desolate, the air damp without the corrective force of the sun. My yoga class gets skipped and I'm reluctant to head out into the night for something as insignificant as a social drink. The very thought of driving seems nightmarish – those impenetrable roads, their edges uncertain; the dance you have to perform with the full beam, flicking it on and off, on and off. Far better to stay at home.

I don't mind staying in at all. I realise that, for plenty of people, it feels like a brutal restriction of their freedom, but it suits me down to the ground. Winter is a quiet house in lamplight, stepping into the garden to see bright stars on a clear night, the roar of the wood-burning stove, and the accompanying smell of charred wood. It is warming the teapot and making cups of bitter cocoa; it is stews magicked from bones with dumplings floating like clouds. It is reading quietly, and passing away the afternoon twilight watching movies. It is thick socks and the bundle of a cardigan.

In summer, I probably average six or seven hours' sleep a night, but in winter it's closer to nine. As soon as the sun goes down, I start thinking about going to bed. Early nights are a habit inherited from my mother's side; none of us are night owls, but neither are we particularly larks. We all just *need* to sleep. I have travelled through distinct phases in my attitude to this: as a child, I found it highly congenial that my grandparents tucked themselves up at the same time as me; as a young adult, I thought it was hilariously tame. As I got older, I found my own urge to sleep more and more inconvenient, and dreamed of unlocking the extra time that, say, a five-hour night would bring. Becoming a parent cured me of that. Some people thrive on a little sleep deprivation, but I do not. I now know that I can achieve far more after nine hours than I can in the spare time afforded by a short night. Sleeping is my sanity, my luxury, my addiction. I'm fairly certain that my decision not to have a second child rests squarely on my worship of sleep.

And winter sleeps are the best. I like my duvet thick and my bedroom cold, so that I have a chill to snuggle against. Unlike those terrible, wrestling summer nights when the room is always too close to allow that final descent into oblivion, the cool air affords deep sleep, and long, magical dreams. Waking in the night, the dark seems more profound and velvety than usual, almost infinite. Winter is a season that invites me to rest well and feel restored, when I am allowed to retreat and be quietly separate.

But in recent weeks, my happy hibernation has been disrupted. I've come to call it the 'terrible threes': the dark insomniac hours when my mind declares itself, fully fired, in the middle of the night. It always happens at 3am: a long way past late, but too early just to surrender and start the day. There, in the truest night, I lie in the dark and catastrophise.

Tonight, I wake from a dream in which I have been loaded into a giant wicker man, ready for burning. It's a lurid fantasy, so gothic in its sense of persecution that I finding myself laughing at it in the silence. What a silly little human I am, to dream such obvious things and then wake up with my heart pounding and my throat tight. Still, it stops me from falling back to sleep. This cliché has produced a very real physical effect. I am alert to its threat. I shift against my pillows, vigilant.

I turn onto my side, plump my pillows, take a swig of water from the bottle I keep beside me. The night goes on. I could make a career out of worrying, if only anyone would pay me. What do I worry about in these long nights? Money. Death. Failure. The familiar horsemen of those quiet apocalypses that only happen when the sun's gone down. In the middle of the night, I can worry my house onto the edge of a cliff, forever about to topple onto the rocks below. I am only ever a missed wage packet away from total annihilation. I carry too much debt. I own nothing. I have nothing to show for my forty-odd years on this earth, except for a pile of dusty books.

Yet here I am, inching even closer to the abyss, throwing away the secure underpinnings of my life by leaving my secure job. In daylight, I can make an account of the stress that made the decision to leave a sensible one; the slow encroachment that ate into my family life. But that's in the daytime, when I value such things as calm and freedom. In the dark, I am struck by a dyspeptic bout of conservatism. I should have a savings account containing a year's salary. I should have proper life insurance. I have squandered something, somehow. I am not sure what, or when, but I despise myself for it. The precariousness of my life bites me hard. I can feel its teeth in my gut. I am nothing, I am no one, I have failed.

4am. The ego flares like a struck match: bright, blue, fleeting. I am thankful to be alone when this happens, to let it burn out in private. We should sometimes be grateful for the solitudes of night, of a winter. They save us from displaying our worst selves to the waking world.

I turn again, adjust the covers, gulp more water. Two whiskies, drunk late and in desolation, announce their presence in my temples. I should have known better, but I always go and make it worse. There's no denying that a stiff drink will lead you by the hand to sleep, but it's a restless bedfellow, and tends to wake again in the red-eye hours before dawn.

I will not sleep now. It's a fool's errand to try. I can feel my heart beating beneath the duvet, my breath failing to fill my lungs. I sit on the edge of the bed and find my slippers with cold feet. I rub my eyes, and grope for my glasses.

I pad downstairs to find my notebook.

★

Hazel Ryan opens a wooden box and hunts through the wood shavings and straw.

'Yes,' she says, 'here she is.'

She plunges in her hand and pulls out a ball of yellow fur about the size of a walnut. A hibernating dormouse. It is round and compact, with its tiny pink feet tucked in to its belly, its ears pressed back, and its black-tipped tail folded up over its head, as if to tie the whole arrangement in place. Hazel places the dormouse into the palm of my hand, and it rolls like a marble. It is lighter than air, and surprisingly cold, but also soft and slightly squishy. You couldn't mistake it for dead. It is in the deepest of sleeps, drowsing until the summer.

Only three native mammals hibernate in the UK: bats, hedgehogs and dormice. Other species, like frogs and badgers, go into a state of torpor on cold days, dropping their body temperature and slowing their breathing and heart rate to conserve energy for short periods of time. But true hibernation – when this cooling and slowing happens for extended periods of time, and is not responsive to the outside temperature or the immediate availability of food – is relatively rare.

Dormice don't work to a strict timetable; their hibernation is dependent on the weather. They spend the early autumn building up reserves of the liquid brown fat that makes them squishy to the touch – as Hazel shows me, you can leave fingerprints on a hibernating dormouse, so fluid is the layer of fat underneath its skin. This is an easily accessible energy store to get them through the long months to come. So from September, they gorge on hedgerow fruits like blackberries, hazelnuts and chestnuts in an attempt to double their bodyweight from around 15–20g to a rotund 40g. They have to do this quickly, at the rate of around one gram a day. In times of abundance, they can become obese. In times of scarcity, they will try to delay hibernation until they're plump enough to survive.

But when the first frosts arrive, they need to be ready. Dormice have a high surface area to volume ratio, which means that they can lose heat very quickly. The extra fat makes them lethargic anyway. In the last few days before hibernation, they build their nest, a tight ball of moss, bark and leaves. In the summer, they live in trees, but the temperature fluctuation is too great up high, so their hibernation nests are built in dips in the ground, perhaps around the roots of a tree. They aim to create an environment that collects rain and dew, so that the nest stays damp through winter. This sounds far from cosy to the human mind, but for dormice it's an essential element of their survival: they are so small, that, without external moisture, they would desiccate during their long sleep.

The right location found, they bundle themselves tightly into their nest and seal up the opening: 'If you can't find a door,' says Hazel, 'there's a dormouse in it.' They tend to hibernate individually, but a recent radio-tracking study found some evidence of nest sharing. This may happen when there's less choice of habitat. Dormice will seek out the perfect climate, and if there aren't many sites available, this may force them to share – in captivity, sharing becomes more common.

Safely in their hibernation nest, the dormice will lower their body temperature to that of their surroundings, which is usually 5°C or less. To hibernate efficiently, they should be just above freezing. If they warm to 6°C, their metabolic rate increases and they start to burn fat; below zero, they also need to call on their fat reserves to avoid freezing. If they manage to hit the right temperature, they will hibernate from October to May, slowing down their metabolic rate, breathing very slowly and matching the temperature of the outside world until the first days of summer, when there are enough insects to feed on again. Even after they wake, they will fall into periods of torpor when food is scarce; for example, when it's raining or during the 'hungry gap' between their preferred crops. Dormice spend more time in hibernation than they spend awake.

I had always imagined hibernation as one long monotonous sleep, but Hazel tells me that in fact dormice wake up around every ten days, staying in their nests, but bringing their metabolism up to speed again for a short period of time. It is thought that this allows their kidneys to flush out toxins, and also provides an important opportunity to check that their nest is still safe. Hazel is the Chief Conservation Officer at the Wildwood Trust in Kent, and the dormice that she looks after are often underweight as they head into winter – quite often they are from orphaned litters, or ones that were mistimed with the seasons. Others have been accidentally dug up in their nests. Because they are at a greater risk of not surviving their hibernation, they are unravelled from their cosy beds at regular intervals to be weighed, and this is what I'm witnessing now. I would love to claim I'm helping, but I think I'm actually just getting in the way and cooing a lot.

It's hard to think of anything more objectively cute than a dormouse: tiny, soft and sleepy, they seem almost primed to invite human adoration. They are also extremely vulnerable: the population of hazel dormice has been declining for some time, and they're now considered to be in danger of extinction. The world has turned, and dormice have been left behind. Seasons are shifting, hedgerows and woodland habitats are being lost, and their food sources are disappearing. They may be too fragile to survive in the industrialised world, but for now they remain an icon of indolence, drowsing away the winter as if oblivious to the future.

★

Downstairs at 4am, I set to work. It felt like an act of mania to get up in the middle of the night, but with a hot cup of tea in my hand, it seems more like an urge towards sanity. Now that I'm upright, my thoughts settle like a snow globe. Everything falls back into perspective.

I clear the surface of my desk and make a pool of light with my lamp. I go off to fetch matches and light a candle. One light is steady and sure, the other uncertain and flickering. I open my notebook and work between these two poles. On balance, it's where I prefer to be: somewhere in the middle. Certainty is a dead space, in which there's no more room to grow. Wavering is painful. I'm glad to be travelling between the two.

I've come to love this part of the night, the almost-morning, which feels exclusively mine. Being the only one awake makes it a luxurious space in which I can drink in the silence. It's an undemanding moment in the 24-hour cycle, in which nobody can reasonably expect you to be checking texts or emails, and the scrolling feeds of social media have fallen quiet. In a world where it's hard to feel alone, this, finally, is solitude. Even the cats know it's too early to demand to be fed. They raise an ear as I pass, and retreat back into their curled balls.

This is a time in which only a few activities seem right. Mostly, I read at this hour, roaming through the pile of books that live by my favourite chair, waiting to offer up fragments of learning, rather than inviting cover-to-cover pursuits. I will browse a chapter here, a segment there, or hunt through an index for a matter that's on my mind. I love the loose, exploratory reading that happens in the night, free of the day's obligations. For once, I am not reading to seek escape; instead, having already made my getaway, I am able to roam through the free, extra space I've found, being as restless and impatient as I like, revelling in the play of my own absorption. They say that we should dance like no one is watching. I think that applies to reading, too.

The inky hours are also for writing: the scratch and flow of pen on good paper, the stuttering chains of words that expand to fill pages and pages. Sometimes writing is a race against your own mind, as your hand labours to keep up with the flood tide of your thoughts, and I feel that most acutely at night, when there are no competing demands on my attention. That slightly sleepy, dazed state erodes the barriers of my waking brain. My dreams are still present, like an extra dimension to my perception. But crucially, my sensible daytime self, bossy and overbearing, still slumbers. Without its overseeing eye, I can see different futures and make imaginative leaps. I can confess all my sins to a piece of paper, with no one to censor it.

I write on screen, too, in the night, with the brightness turned down to a muted glow. I find that I can churn out thousands of words like this, falling deep into concentration and letting my hands talk without the interference of my consciousness.

If my night-waking feels elemental to me, then perhaps that is because it was once a normal component of human sleep, only recently forgotten. In *At Day's Close*, the historian A. Roger Ekirch argues that, before the industrial revolution, it was normal to divide the night into two periods of sleep: the 'first', or 'dead', sleep, lasting from the evening until the early hours of the morning; and the 'second', or 'morning', sleep, which took the slumberer safely to daybreak. In between, there was an hour or more of wakefulness known as the 'watch', in which 'Families rose to urinate, smoke tobacco, and even visit close neighbours. Many made love, prayed, and … reflected on their dreams, a significant source of solace and self-awareness.' In the intimacy of the darkness, families and lovers could hold deep, rich, roaming conversations that had no place in the busy daytime.

This was a function of the times in which the night really was dark, when the poor would go to sleep early to save the price of candles, and even the rich would have the choice of struggling on with their occupations in limited light, or surrendering to sleep. Outside the house, the streets were usually unlit, so the only navigable space was home.

However, this was so ordinary (and perhaps also so private a moment in the day), that little is written about it. Ekirch picks up a range of passing references to the first and second sleeps in diaries, letters and literature, but this ancient practice is nearly invisible to the contemporary eye. A 1996 study by Thomas Wehr and colleagues attempted to replicate the conditions of winter sleep in prehistoric times, depriving subjects of artificial light for fourteen hours each night, and observing what happened to their sleep patterns. After several weeks, the participants fell into a pattern of lying awake in bed for two hours before falling asleep for around four hours. They would then wake up and enjoy two or three hours of time that was characterised as contemplative and restful, and then take another four hours of sleep until morning. Most interesting of all, Wehr observed that the mid-night watch was far from an anxious time for his subjects. They felt calm and reflective in these moments, and blood tests revealed elevated levels of prolactin, the hormone that stimulates the production of breast milk in nursing mothers. In most men and women, prolactin levels tend to be low, but the watch seemed to have 'an endocrinology all of its own', which

Wehr compared to an altered state of consciousness similar to meditation.

In this borderland between wake and sleep, it's tempting to believe that our ancestors experienced a different state of being to any we know, or any we *can* know unless we refuse the intrusion of artificial light. Maybe my sleeplessness isn't only caused by anxiety about the future. In the twenty-first century, we are awash with light, not just from the pendants and lamps that deliberately light up our homes in the evening, but also the ever-growing legions of electronic devices that flicker and pulse and glow to tell us that they're doing something. Light, nowadays, can feel like an intruder, always seeming to carry with it a unit of information, or an obligation.

Even left alone on the sideboard, my phone is a restless creature, periodically fidgeting into life to announce a new message, or an update, or a reminder of something I was trying hard to forget. I've spent years attempting to find an alarm clock that lets me check the time without casting light into the room, but I've now given up. The digital LED clock kept me awake with its green glow; the traditional clock with luminous hands proved impossible to read; the 'nightglow' clock that only lit up when I pressed a button felt like it burned my eyeballs in the middle of the night, leaving eerie blue phantoms behind my eyelids when I tried to return to sleep. Add to that my television (yes, I am one of those sinners who loves to drift off to sleep in the company of a panel show), with its piercing red standby light that seems impossible to disable, and the neighbours at the back, who apparently find it necessary to floodlight their garden each evening. Light is inescapable. In my town, the local council is gradually replacing the old, orange-toned sodium lamps with new, brighter LED ones. The dark – and our fears that lurk in it – is pushed ever further back, but residents are complaining that they can't sleep; that the light finds its way past black-out blinds and double-lined curtains.

There is not enough night left for us. We have lost our true instincts for darkness, and its invitation to spend some time in the proximity of our dreams. Our personal winters are so often accompanied by insomnia, but perhaps we are still drawn towards that unique space of intimacy and contemplation, darkness and silence, without really knowing what we're seeking. Perhaps, after all, we are being urged towards our own comfort.

Sleep is not a dead space, but a doorway to a different kind of consciousness – one that is reflective and restorative, full of tangential thought and unexpected insights. In winter, we are invited into a particular

mode of sleep: not a regimented eight hours, moni-
tored by an app and checked against a graph, but a
slow, ambulatory process in which waking thoughts
merge with dreams, and space is made in the blackest
hours to repair the fragmented narratives of our days.

And yet we are pushing it away, this innate skill we
have for digesting the difficult parts of life. My own
mid-night terrors vanish when I turn insomnia into a
watch: a claimed, sacred space in which I have nothing to do but contemplate. Here, I am offered a place
in-between, like finding a hidden door, the stuff of
dreams. Even dormice know how to do it: they wake
a while, and tend to business, before surrendering back
to sleep.

Over and again, we find that winter offers us liminal spaces to inhabit. Yet still we refuse them. The
work of the cold season is to learn to welcome them.

DECEMBER

LIGHT

'My husband calls it "preparing for the apoca-lypse",' says Grania O'Brien. 'But otherwise I'll just burrito myself in the duvet all day.'

My sneaking affection for winter is, by now, no secret, but I accept that most people find winter a bit of a drag, forcing them to shelter inside from the weather. For some, though, winter is a season of misery. Grania has Seasonal Affective Disorder, or SAD, a form of depression that arrives with the shortening days. It can bring about feelings of sad-ness, misery or despair, lethargy, insomnia, anxiety, low concentration levels, and a drop in the immune system. It's also associated with increased appetite, and in particular cravings for carbs, which can mean weight gain over the winter months. Many people with SAD turn to alcohol or drugs to alleviate their symptoms.

'By nature, I'm optimistic and sparkly,' Grania tells me, 'but as the days get shorter, I'm on a short fuse. I have mood swings, and I struggle to concentrate. It's like I lose all clarity of thought; I can't strategise. Left to my own devices, I'd spend most of the winter carb-loading, so I have to stock up the freezer before it all begins. If I can easily eat something healthy, I'm less likely to binge on cakes and chips.'

'So it's the dark,' I ask, 'and not the cold?'

'Oh yes,' she says. 'Good winter light is wonderful, but those days are few and far between, and they're too short when they come. My alarm goes off at six each morning, and in the winter it's still dark. I just can't bring myself to get out of bed. I want to hibernate instead.' Without intervention, she would crawl back under the covers at 4pm, and fall asleep again. It's clear that something very powerful is telling her brain to retreat into some kind of winter stasis.

I ask her if she's always felt this way, and she says that she's never exactly loved winter, but that she began to notice the effects much more strongly as an adult, when she was responsible for motivating herself through the darker months. It's not clear what actually causes SAD. One theory is that circadian rhythms are disrupted by the changing seasons; another is that reduced daylight leads to lowered serotonin levels, which can be a cause of depression. People with SAD possibly produce more melatonin than others, which can cause them to feel more sleepy. Whatever the cause, it seems that SAD is most prevalent in countries like the UK, where the changing seasons bring about marked differences in light exposure across the year.

It's strange to think that something so intangible as light can have such a huge impact on our mood and well-being, until you remember that many parts of the natural world – such as dormice and trees – respond very strongly to the amount of light they receive. Electric light may now be abundant, but sunlight – the only light that our bodies have evolved to use – is hard to come by. In summer, we increasingly hide from it, working in air-conditioned offices and layering on the sunblock to protect us from the effects of ageing and burning, and, ultimately, skin cancer. For my own part, this regime starts as soon as the days start to warm up again in the spring; I have been known to burn in February. In winter, we find it ever easier to avoid the ravages of the weather outside, piling into cars, shopping in covered malls, and exercising in gyms.

But sunlight is one of the key ways in which we synthesise vitamin D, along with eating oily fish (another declining habit), eggs and meat, and supplementing it through fortified foods and vitamin pills. The British winter months, from October to March, have never contained enough UVB radiation to enable the production of vitamin D, but many of us are no longer getting enough in the summer, either, and our children are beginning to feel the effects. A clinical review paper by Professor Simon Pearce and Dr Tim Cheetham, published in the *BMJ* in January 2010, found that there has been a resurgence in childhood rickets, the disease that causes weak, soft bones and perhaps even skeletal deformities.

It is yet another impossible aspect of modern life that we must now simultaneously worry about our children coming in to contact with the sun, and not coming in to contact with it enough; yet another one of those balances that we must now work to achieve, because the knowledge is out there, and the world has changed. So, on top of worrying about the calories we consume, and the exact composition of those calories, and whether we are getting enough exercise, and how we can reduce the waste packaging that inevitably comes with our food, and whether we're recycling enough, and managing stress and being saintly enough towards our children and saintly enough towards ourselves, we must now also ensure that we're getting just the right dose of sunshine. It's part of the new payload of worry that makes every day feel that little bit more wintery.

Supplementing vitamin D appears to help some people with Seasonal Affective Disorder, but the evidence is largely anecdotal. According to a 2005 research overview by Kathryn A. Roecklein and Kelly J. Rohan, light therapy improves symptoms in over 50 per cent of cases, and this percentage rises if the therapy is combined with antidepressants. Again, there has been little conclusive research into how this works, but the correct sources of artificial light have been shown to stimulate the body's production of its own vitamin D. It's as if the raw fact of the vitamin is not enough; it's the process that's important, the experience of bathing in light. And this is what Grania shows me, when she talks about how she's learned to cope with her SAD: bright pools of light, all through her home.

First, she takes me to her bedroom, where she is now woken every morning by an alarm clock that imitates the rising sun: glowing softly at first, then gradually reaching the intensity of full daylight, allowing her to wake up slowly and to avoid that grim battle against the self in darkness at 6am. She uses bright lightbulbs through the whole house, and keeps the place lit up all day, regardless of the time; she lights fires at night and goes walking at lunchtime, forcing herself outside to encounter as much of the day as she can.

But the adaptation that fascinates me the most is a rectangular device that sits by her desk, looking for all the world like an iPad. When she switches it on, it glows at 10,000 lux, simulating the full blast of daylight at the height of summer. She sits at her computer to show me what it does, and it looks like nothing, really: just a bright light in a room that's already subject to a skylight and a lightbulb at midday. But the effect, for Grania, is enormous. She is bathed in a pearlescent wash of the right frequencies of light, at the right intensity. A smile eases across her face.

★

> 'Tis the year's midnight, and it is the day's,
> Lucy's, who scarce seven hours herself unmasks;
> > The sun is spent, and now his flasks
> > Send forth light squibs, no constant rays;
> > The world's whole sap is sunk;
> The general balm th' hydroptic earth hath drunk,
> Whither, as to the bed's feet, life is shrunk,
> Dead and interr'd; yet all these seem to laugh,
> Compar'd with me, who am their epitaph.

John Donne's poem 'A Nocturnal upon St Lucy's Day', is perhaps the perfect reading for the seasonally affected. A grief-stricken love song to a deceased lover, it rings with a kind of midwinter melancholy. Donne's poems are notoriously difficult to date, but this one is often thought to be a response to the death of his wife, Anne, in 1617, following the birth of their twelfth child. It is certainly a poem of utter desolation, as the speaker imagines himself entirely spent and unable to recover from his loss: 'I am none; nor will my sun renew.'

However, it is also a poem of profound intimacy, where 'the day's deep midnight' brings about a kind of communion with his lost partner, and in which we are invited to share a glimpse into the parts of their union that others might seek to hide, and which many of us would not expect to miss:

> Oft a flood
> Have we two wept, and so
> Drown'd the whole world, us two; oft did we grow
> To be two chaoses, when we did show
> Care to aught else; and often absences
> Withdrew our souls, and made us carcasses.

The metaphysics of this poem position love as a medium of transformation, creating 'a quintessence even from nothingness', but, after death, possessing the same power of transformation in reverse, leaving the speaker 're-begot/Of absence, darkness, death: things which are not.' Yet somehow, amid all this blackness, there are hints of optimism to be found. Love, here, has such power that it seems worth the pain of its ending. And, in the final stanza, we find Donne addressing the next generation of young lovers, for whom 'the Goat is run/To fetch new lust'. The life cycle continues; love renews. 'Enjoy your summer all', he says, as he prepares for 'Both the year's, and the day's deep midnight'.

The choice of St Lucy's Day is significant here. These days, many Northern European countries mark her feast on 13 December, but in Donne's time it was celebrated on the winter solstice, the shortest day of the year, amid the oppressive darkness. It marked the beginning of Christmastide, and then, as now, the experience of grief must surely have been heightened in times of former high spirits, when those in mourning can feel at their most isolated.

St Lucy herself carries symbolic weight. Her name is associated with the Latin word for light (*lux*, or *lucis* in the plural), and one common story is that she was a third-century martyr during the 'Great Persecution' of the Christians in the Roman Empire, who brought food to those who were hiding in the catacombs of Rome. To keep her hands free for her duties, she wore a crown of candles so that she could see her way through the darkness. This story is still represented in various Nordic churches, when the annual Sankta Lucia service involves a young woman in a white gown, red sash and crown of candles leading a procession of women and girls.

The alternative story of St Lucy is darker still. This Lucia was a young woman from Sicily in the third century AD, who refused to give up her virginity by marrying a pagan nobleman, having consecrated herself to God. Her prospective husband denounced her to the Roman authorities for being a Christian, and the Roman authorities, in turn, threatened to send her to a brothel if she didn't renounce her faith. Lucia refused, and when the authorities attempted to remove her to the brothel, they found that she could not be shifted. Eventually, after a team of oxen had failed to drag her one inch, they stacked kindling around her instead and burned her. But nothing could extinguish Lucy's voice, which chimed on through the flames, proclaiming her faith. A solider stuck a spear through her throat to stop her, but still the words came. Later versions of the story say that her eyes were gouged out too; another says that she gouged them out herself after they were admired by a suitor. Lucy is a symbol of absolute faith and utter purity, but the sins for which she suffers are not her own. Instead, she shoulders the weight of the male gaze, and is destroyed by it.

So Lucy dwells in the darkness of the catacombs, or in the dark of blindness; she brings the light of the martyr's pyre, or the light of a crown of candles. In Donne's poem, she is almost certainly a symbol of female sacrifice for love, but she is also a figurehead for that moment, at the darkest point, when there is a little light remaining.

★

Svenska Kyrkan (Swedish Church) in London's Marylebone is bustling with families. Children eat apple slices and finger sandwiches from plastic tubs, and stand on the pews to get a better look. Toddlers fidget on the laps of their embarrassed parents, and babies reach their arms to transfer from grandfather to grandmother, from father to aunt. Some wear crowns of battery-powered candles. The child next to me is methodically picking the lights out of his and dropping them onto the floor. Today, the church is their domain, and they know it. They're expecting a moment of magic, and they're too excited to sit still. The assembled congregation of Swedish expats eye them indulgently, lean between rows to gossip, and take selfies to send home.

I am in sitting in an unfamiliar church on a Saturday afternoon in the run-up to Christmas, but I'm grateful to be here. It gives me something to do and somewhere to be. Yesterday, I went into the university where I've worked for the last five years, and cleared my office. My notice period was up; my final term was over. I packed my books into boxes, two bookcases' worth, most of them scholarly tomes containing theoretical positions that I suspect I'll never need to adopt again. If I had any sense, I would have left them in the corridor and attached a sign saying 'Take Me'. Still, I tucked them carefully and safely away, wanting to keep them pristine. They are sitting in my front room now, stacked in boxes, while I wait to find out what my new life will be.

I'm an interloper here, sitting alone in the corner of the church amid a sea of families, feeling conspicuously English, and conspicuously a tourist. If I'd realised what a multi-generational affair this would be, I would have brought my own wriggling child with me, if nothing else just to blend in. This is the annual Sankta Lucia service, so popular that it's now ticketed and performed across several dates in mid-December. I try not to look too fascinated at the parts of the experience that are so exotically Swedish to me: the ranks of psalters marked 'psalmboken'; the sea of blond heads. Waiting outside, people were actually eating open sandwiches. Even sitting in the nave, the scent of cardamom and cinnamon – those staples of Swedish baking – wafts up from the basement, and along with it the promise of *fika* – coffee and buns – after the service.

When the priest stands, there is a mass shushing, a pointing at seats and a rash of significant looks spreading across the room. For the briefest moment, we fall silent. A quiet, fatherly man stands before us and says in Swedish, and then in English, 'Do we have any children here today?' The noise rises again. Hands are raised. He smiles. 'Well, I will try my best to help you to know what all this is about.'

He points to the candles on the altar, and lights a third in his hand, telling a carefully sanitised version of the life of Sankta Lucia, who made sacrifices for her faith in God. Lucy's martyrdom is not his point today; instead, he wants us to think about the simple gestures by which we can bring light into the world. 'Every one of us is a lit candle,' he says.

We remain seated to sing two short hymns, and I try to join in, feeling as though my cover is blown. My ignorance of Swedish pronunciation seems to make my voice clang out against the general hum, even though I am only singing in a whisper. But the songs are mercifully short and reasonably paced, and soon we are folding our service sheets again, and the sense of expectation is rising.

The church bells ring and the lights dim. Children whisper, 'Lucia.' More shushing, and then singing fades in, ghostly in the darkness. Heads turn, and a sea of mobile phones light up to catch the spectacle. And soon, here it is: first, the choir mistress walking backwards, conducting. And then, proceeding down the aisle, Lucia. She is wearing a crown of candles – real ones, blazing high – and a long, white dress with a red sash to symbolise her martyrdom. Behind her are fourteen attendants, dressed in the same white, but with laurel wreaths around their heads and candles in their hands. They pool in front of the altar and continue their song: *Stiger med tända ljus / Sankta Lucia, Sankta Lucia!*

Walking with lit candles, Saint Lucy. The tune lilts and chimes like a carousel organ, familiar yet also deeply other. Somebody else's song for somebody else's festival. I'm not sure what Swedish music ought to sound like (ABBA?), but this isn't it; it's too rich and operatic. That's possibly because it was appropriated from a traditional Neapolitan song, a romantic ode to the Borgo Santa Lucia in the Gulf of Naples, describing the pleasures of sailing a boat on the calm seas on a quiet evening.

The Nordic countries seem to have straightforwardly borrowed its title and applied it to a different Saint Lucy. In this version, we are transported to a dark night in which Sankta Lucia walks through the house with candles, returning light to the world. Lucia is not really a martyr in this hymn, killed in bloody and elaborate ways as she protests her union with God. She is a girl in white, who brings light in the darkest hour. She is, in herself, a lit candle.

The choir sings a suite of odes to Saint Lucy, before ending with 'Silent Night', and then proceeding back along the aisle, and fading into silence again. The priest attempts a final address, but he's no match for Lucy. Everybody is talking now, and pulling on coats, ready for the promised coffee and buns downstairs. For my own part, I feel that my time as a tourist in this most beautiful of Christmas services is at an end. To stay on would leave me truly rumbled. I drop a few coins into the collection bag, and make my way back into the grey December afternoon.

As I descend the stairs into Baker Street station, I realise how uplifted I have been by Sankta Lucia, not just the song and the gentle light, but also an hour sat in a church pew, with nothing to do but listen and smile at the occasional fidgeting toddler. It makes me realise that I have been avoiding all society, skulking at home in a kind of shame. I am staying away from others because I don't know what the New Year will bring, and I'm afraid, and I don't have the grace to conceal it. To fill the time, I've been busy doing nothing, giving the outward appearance of purpose while I'm really just scrolling through my phone.

But sitting quietly in church has done me good. My job was to do nothing but listen, and feel, and contemplate, and it was a liberation. I remember too well my own wriggling, bored childhood battles against a church pew, but today, as an adult, I gained something new: a sense of welcome insignificance amid a congregation of people; a lifting of the obligation to endlessly do, if just for an hour; a gentle truce with myself.

I spent most of that time on the verge of tears. I only needed to open up that tiny space to see how black it all was, how close I had come to my mid-winter. Saint Lucy didn't cure me. I didn't dance back up the aisle, having miraculously found my way. But she brought a little light. Just enough to see by.

MIDWINTER

THE ALARM ON MY PHONE trills at a quarter to five and I climb out of an unfamiliar bed and pull on my clothes: thermal vest, long johns, jeans, t-shirt, jumper. Ski socks under walking boots. I have a warm coat, scarf, mittens and hat already packed in the boot of the car.

I meet my friend downstairs in her kitchen, making a pot of tea. We gulp it quietly, worrying about the traffic. Are we leaving early enough? We'd better get going. We ease our respective children out of bed, and follow the ritual all over again: socks, long johns, vests, jeans, jumpers. We wrap them in blankets and whisper to them that they can sleep in the car, knowing full well that they will not.

Setting off at a quarter past five, we drive towards Amesbury in the pitch black, the kids growing in-creasingly rowdy in the back of the car. There's a steady stream of traffic heading towards the South West, perhaps an unusual amount for 22 December, but then again, perhaps not. Perhaps it's the beginning of the Christmas exodus back home to visit family. Either way, I was expecting more: a crowd of pilgrims heading to Stonehenge, a massing of people from across the country, all drawn to this icon of ancestral worship on the morning of the winter solstice. But there are no more cars entering the site than you'd find on an average afternoon. It is, I suppose, six o'clock in the morning, and pitch black outside. But still, I was secretly hoping for something a little more anarchic, something that thrilled against my bland sense of middle-class agnosticism.

I attended a Christmas party last night, and whenever I mentioned where we were heading today, I would invariably receive a nervous chuckle, a sneer, or a sucking in of breath. *The solstice? With the crusties? The tree-huggers? The hippies? The Druids?* It was clear that I was about to do something ever so slightly embarrassing: to join in the marking of an invisible point in the year in the company of the New Age crowd, with their daft rituals and invented religion. 'You're not one of them, are you?' asked one man. I assured him that I was not.

The iconic ring of standing stones that make up Stonehenge is thought to have been constructed between 4,000 and 5,000 years ago. For the most part, the circle is composed of trilithons, which are two upright stones with a third stone forming a lintel across the top. They're part of a wider complex of Neolithic and Bronze Age monuments in the surrounding Wiltshire countryside, which include several hundred burial mounds. Standing four metres high, they're a commanding sight in the landscape, and it is clear that they had ritual significance, although the exact nature of that ritual and belief has been lost to time.

Geoffrey of Monmouth, writing his *Historia Regum Britanniae* in the twelfth century, thought the stones had healing properties, and suggested that they were brought to the site by Merlin and Uther Pendragon on the instruction of King Aurelius Ambrosius, who wanted to commemorate a battle against the Saxons. He thought that it was originally built in Ireland by a race of giants, and he noted that 15,000 knights could not shift the stones, but Merlin could, using his particular cunning.

In the early eighteenth century, the antiquarian William Stukeley analysed the surrounding earthworks and suggested that Stonehenge was in fact a Druidic site of worship. He envisioned the rituals that took place there based on scant historical sources, mostly Roman, which portrayed Druids as mystical savages, both disturbingly other and also feeble in the face of an organised military force. It appears that Stukeley invented as much as he revealed, but he created a sense of fascination with the site, and started to identify as a Druid himself, taking on the name Chyndonax, which he believed to be Druidic. Stonehenge was to become a popular attraction for the Victorians, who would visit in their thousands at midsummer to see the sun rise. At the time, tourists were given a chisel and encouraged to chip off their own personal souvenir from the monument.

Despite various academic debunkings of the Druidic connection, the association has stuck, and the twentieth century saw Stonehenge growing as a site of significance to present-day Druids and other pagan groups, at a time when society at large has increasingly sought to protect and preserve its heritage. This has frequently led to conflict. Access to the stones was first restricted in 1978, amid fears of erosion as visitor numbers grew. In 1985, there was a violent confrontation between New Age travellers and the police, after the site was closed to people seeking to attend the annual midsummer Stonehenge Free Festival. The 'exclusion zone' around the stones continued until 1999, when campaigners obtained a ruling from the European Court of Human Rights, which confirmed Stonehenge as a place of worship, and asserted the right of diverse groups including spiritualists, pagans and Druids to worship there. As the ban was lifted, English Heritage urged that solstice celebrations remain peaceful and respectful, and there has been no trouble reported since that time. Stonehenge might now be seen as not only a symbol of the clash of cultures, but also of their pragmatic reconciliation.

Apart from their long history, the reason for the continued meaning placed on the stones lies in their astronomical alignment. At midsummer each year, the longest day begins with the sun rising behind the Heel Stone and then shining straight into the heart of the circle. At midwinter, the shortest day once ended with the sun setting between the two upright stones of the tallest trilithon in the circle. This is no longer standing, so now the celebration takes place on the following morning, marking the sunrise as the days finally begin to lengthen. This is what we have come to see: the spectacle of the returning of the light, and the celebration that accompanies it.

I'm not entirely sure what I was expecting to find here at midwinter, but the reality is certainly tamer. We queue in the English Heritage cafe behind jolly men and women in late middle age, most of whom look as though they just stepped out of Marks & Spencer, although some are wearing cloaks. One man has donned a Green Man mask, his features disguised by a pile of nylon oak leaves. There is a sense of polite leisure in the air. The cafe has stocked its fridges with nettle wine and mead, but nobody seems to be drinking. We might as well be queuing in the Women's Institute tent at the local village fete.

I order sausage rolls and hot chocolate for the kids, and we sit outside in the surprisingly mild night, wondering when we should make our way along to the henge. As the kids begin to run out of patience, we board a shuttle bus that says 'To The Stones', and our fellow passengers make a cosy, grandparental fuss of the children. Then, we are released to get our first glimpse of Stonehenge, with the sky clearing to dark blue in advance of sunrise.

There's a crowd of people already milling around the stones, and they're certainly not the English Heritage gift-shop sort; in fact, it feels more like the bitter end of a rock festival, complete with the compulsory good-natured police officers, and first aiders on hand to support drug casualties. I ask one of them if she's expecting much business, and she tells me that it's quiet at the winter solstice; all-night partying is more of a midsummer thing. There are people in Peruvian ponchos; dreadlocked New Age travellers; women in long medieval gowns; a man in a silver space suit, playing a melodica. Music drifts from all around: a host of different drums, a singing bowl, a few chords on a squeezebox. People dance along, or stand to watch.

We are buffeted by a hobby horse, someone dressed in concentric rings draped in multi-coloured rags. He looks as though he's lost his Morris side.

It's an almost bewildering mix of cultures, and I feel awkward among them, if only because I lack their exuberance. There are a few families looking a lot like us, slightly embarrassed in our dowdy outdoor wear, and not quite sure how to join in with the celebration, or whether we want to. Our instinct is to tell the children off for getting too close to the stones, rather than to invite them to commune with them. We're interlopers here, but I'm not sure what interloper means in this context. There's certainly no sense in which we're not welcome, and the crowd is too diverse for us to truly stand out. If simply wanting to spend the solstice in close proximity to the stones is enough of a reason, then we're not interlopers at all. I just don't know how to worship in this way.

The object here is ecstasy, and not the kind that the first aiders are monitoring. Some people are seeking it through movement and sound; others standing quietly, their eyes closed, touching the stones. I can certainly understand that hit: being able to get up close to the trilithons, to touch them and truly sense their height and bulk, is an awe-inducing privilege, and one attained at the mere cost of an early morning. When I've seen them before, from the safe confines of the tourist path, they've always looked small to me, uniform, even slightly underwhelming. Today they are none of these things; they are not even grey, but green and yellow with lichens, full of crevices and protrusions. You can imagine them being cut from a quarry, shaped, hefted over land, and positioned just-so by human hands. It's a wonder to be here, to pick up their damp scent, and to get a sense of their organisation.

I weave between them into the inner circle, which is now growing more and more crowded with people dressed in red. Something is about to happen: you can feel the expectation rising. By my watch, I make it ten minutes until sunrise. The drumming has intensified; from somewhere, there are wafts of smoke. We round up the children, and I haul Bert onto my shoulders to see. The press of bodies has grown denser. We can get no closer now than the outer sarsen stones, and from the middle there is singing. I can just about catch the harmonies but not the words. It's stirring, nonetheless. I feel as though I'm standing at the edge of a temple rather than an archaeological site, but it's chaotic, and slightly high. The drumming builds and quickens, frantic hands finding a beat, phrases sung ever more fervently. I can't see much; I doubt anybody can. There's no order of service or hymn sheet, no sense that we're all expected to be thinking the same things, or even to be here for the same reasons. The glorious jumble leaves me slightly confused, but mostly elated.

At some indistinct point, the grey pre-dawn fades into bright white, and the sun is up, albeit invisibly behind a bank of cloud. People – whoever they are, from whichever tribe – shake hands and hug and say, 'We have turned the year!' We do it too, much to the bafflement of the children, who are now immersed in a fantasy in which the stones are dragons, and they are their keepers. There is no distinct moment of release. It's reminiscent of a missed orgasm; that long, intent, breath-holding build-up that comes to nothing much. The significance is the same either way. Light is coming back into the world, after months of encroaching darkness.

I stay near the circle long after it's light, hoping that the clouds will clear and I'll get to glimpse that golden ball framed by standing stones, but it's not to be. We walk back to the visitor centre through the surrounding barrows, and it's all over.

*

There's a standard take on moments like this: good old English eccentrics, a bit daft, and a bit embarrassing, but harmless really. We're not keen, as a nation, on expressions of mass exuberance, unless it's related to football. We're suspicious of the donning of robes, of the desire towards ritual. We like our belief tempered with an apologetic quality, a signal of humility. Sermons must bore us. Prayers must be muttered. Singing must be undertaken as a grim obligation, mumbled in the quietest possible voice, by people maintaining strict personal boundaries. The seeking of ecstasy doesn't come into it.

The following day, I scan the news coverage to see what I ought to have made of it all. A few of the papers carry photographs of grotesque, wild-looking people in strange costumes, hugging stones. The BBC focuses on a parking dispute of which I was entirely unaware. The *Daily Star* says that we all 'descended' on Stonehenge, as if we formed a mass invasion force from the air. AccuWeather claims that the invisible sunrise was 'spectacular'. It's hard not to think that all the copy was written in advance, and pushed out online without much thought, existing only to satisfy readers who will tut and shake their heads at the idiocy of these weirdos.

There are already videos, too. The comments section on YouTube is a pit of condescension and hellfire-and-brimstone evangelism, with a smattering of racism thrown in: 'THIS IS PURE SATANIC!' shouts one; 'heathens,' spits another; 'these are hippies, don't compare it to our Slavic ancestors,' says a third. 'Fake pagans'; 'bunch of crack heads'; 'I smell marijuana'. (For the record, I didn't.)

What I saw at Stonehenge didn't strike me as offensive in any way. Maybe some of it didn't suit my personal taste, and some of it left me wondering what was the connection between the place, the belief and the action. But those things were none of my business, and not a single person made it their business to ask why I was there. Certainly, it represented a jumble of different spiritualities, but that struck me as profoundly tolerant. Here was a group of people who were willing to share their chosen place of worship, and to respect each other's mode of celebration. They didn't seek the bullying voice of consistency or conformity; they didn't denounce each other as following a divergent path. They just did their thing, and let others do theirs.

More and more, I find that I'm drawn to moments like this: an uplift in the monotonous progress of the year, and a way to mark the movement to the next phase. But that desire also makes me squirm, as though it's some kind of perversion that I'm shy to admit in public. Rituals have always seemed a tiny bit daft to me. To need this one – to want it – sits uneasily.

I contact Philip Carr-Gomm, the leader of the Order of Bards, Ovates and Druids, after reading an interview in *The Times* in which he acknowledges the same sense of twitching discomfort. 'I think Druidry is a bit wacky myself,' he says, 'but then a lot of what's going on in the world is wacky. Trump is a bit weird. I look at Anglican bishops in their robes and think they are a bit weird. As John Cleese once said, the greatest fear of the English is embarrassment, so I am saddled with that.'

I, too, am saddled with that: the sense that, rather than being immoral, dangerous or stupid, the creation of rituals to find deeper meaning in the world is simply cringeworthy. Philip laughs kindly when I scrunch up my nose in the process of describing the Stonehenge solstice. He stopped attending a few years ago. He still marks the solstice in a quieter way, but also sees it as a part of a system of celebrations that arrive at regular intervals to make life feel more manageable.

'Druids follow the eight-fold Wheel of the Year,' he says, 'which means that we have something to do every six weeks. It's a useful period of time – you always have the next moment in sight. It creates a pattern through the year.'

As he describes in his book, *Druid Mysteries*, the year is reborn again at the winter solstice, which Druids call Alban Arthan (the Light of Arthur). They hold a ceremony in which they 'cast away whatever impedes the appearance of light', and throw scraps of fabric on the ground in darkness to signify the things which have been holding them back. Then, a single lamp is lit with a flint and raised in the east to welcome a new cycle, which will reach its peak at the summer solstice.

The next festival is Imbolc on the first day of February, when the early snowdrops show. It marks the end of winter, a time when the snow would traditionally melt, and its debris could be cleared away; but it is also the beginning of spring, when the first lambs are born. Soon, the spring equinox comes around, when the days and nights are of equal length and Alban Eilir (Light of the Earth) is celebrated; followed by Beltane on May Day, when spring is in full bloom, and when cattle would traditionally emerge from their winter confinement. This system continues through the summer and eventually we return to Samhain, the dying of the year and the start of the liminal period before it is renewed at the winter solstice. Four solar festivals, linked to solstices and equinoxes, and four pastoral ones in between, celebrating key moments in the lived experience of the year.

'In mainstream culture, the only major festival is now Christmas,' says Philip, 'and perhaps also a summer holiday. The gap is far too long. When you're following a Way like Druidism, the pattern of festivals gives a rhythm to the year, offering a way through even the darkest periods. 'I tune in to winter now at Samhain, knowing that in six weeks' time I've got the solstice, and then in another six weeks, I'm moving into spring. I've got three markers.'

Is this an invented religion, cobbling together borrowed rituals, and harking back to an imagined past where mysticism reigned? Probably. Maybe. But I don't think it matters. It expresses a craving that so many of us will recognise. Have we really got so far into the realm of electric light and central heating that the rhythm of the year is irrelevant to us, and we no longer even want to notice the point at which the nights start getting shorter again? If our current society lacks a way to offer us the meanings we seek, then it's entirely reasonable to reimagine the old ways of doing it, or to create new ones.

★

'Do you pray?' asks author Jay Griffiths in her 2019 essay, 'Daily Grace', published online by *Aeon* magazine. 'Yes, I pray,' she replies to herself, 'earthwise rather than to any off-ground god – and, though I cannot tell you the words I use, I will tell you their core is beauty.'

I may be embarrassed to admit it, but I pray earthwise too. I learned to meditate over a decade ago now, and when motherhood made it sometimes impossible to find the time to sit for twenty minutes, twice a day, I found a way to distil a little of that experience. By closing my eyes, however briefly, and resting my thoughts on the core of my perception, I can gain some of the peace that meditation brings me. I have come to think of it as prayer, although I ask for nothing, and speak to no one within it. It is a profoundly non-verbal experience, a sharp breath of pure being amid a forest of words. It is an untangling, a moment to feel the true ache of desire, the gentle wash of self-compassion, the heart-swell of thanks, the tick tick tick of existence. It is a moment when, alone, I feel at my most connected with others. I can feel entirely separate in a crowd of people, but closing my eyes, I can feel as though I have walked into a river of all consciousness, bathed in common humanity.

I shrink from even writing these words, because I do not have friends who pray like this, or who talk about the world in this sense. I'm ashamed of it. I find myself groping for the basic vocabulary to express what I mean. I flinch away from the certainties of religion, and from the carefully noncommittal language that I find online – the Internet-spiritual, celebrating the moments in which we're blessed and grateful, but reluctant to pin down by whom we're blessed, or to whom we're grateful. I could not, in the tradition of various twelve-step programmes, defer to a higher power without knowing exactly what that higher power constituted, and what they would have me believe, and whether I agree with their principles. I am a profoundly rational being, prone to asking questions. I cannot accept vagueness. I require a systematic understanding of any beliefs that I might hold. I need them to make coherent sense.

But my prayers – earthwise as they are – take me to a place that I am unable to dissect or scrutinise, a space beyond words. When I am not praying, I struggle to imagine a god that I would be willing to pray to, but still I am drawn to prayer for prayer's sake. It is an act that my mind knows, that happens without my intervention. 'Some days, although we cannot pray, a prayer/utters itself' begins Carol Ann Duffy's most famous poem, 'Prayer', which later goes on to show the faithless turning to piano scales and the Shipping Forecast to capture a little of the quality of prayerfulness. Praying is something that I can do, and so I do it. It seems to represent an atavistic impulse on my part, a desire to find life in the world around me, the trees and stones and bodies of water, the birds and mammals that enter my line of sight. Mine is a personal animism, hushed by my conscious brain, nurtured by my unconscious.

But a prayer, at least, is something that happens silently, in secret. It is nothing that I have to advertise or discuss, and so I am able to be discreet about it, disingenuously hanging with the rationalists while I furtively seek the numinous. This urge towards ritual is something new and altogether more risky, because it makes my invisible devotions visible. But I got enormous comfort from sitting in the Swedish Church and listening to the choir, and I got a distinct uplift from merging with the crowd at Stonehenge and being part of the effort to mark the passing of another phase in the year, and the beginning of a new one. Since I attended the Stonehenge solstice, I have noticed things that I don't usually attend to; I have noticed that the sun rises a little earlier every morning, and that it's therefore a little easier to get out of bed. It made a difference to celebrate that change in the presence of others. It added a little joy to that simple act of noticing, and bolstered the dark need that lurked behind it with fellow human spirit. It took away a little of the shame at needing it.

The loose communities that we find in spiritual or religious gatherings were once entirely ordinary to us, but now it seems like it is more radical to join them, a brazen challenge to the strictures of the nuclear family, the tendency to stick within tight friendship groups, the shrinking away from the awe-inspiring. Congregations are elastic, stretching to take in all kinds of people, and bringing up unexpected perspectives and insights. We need them now more than ever.

'Rituals are the doorways of the psyche, between the sacred and the profane, between purity and dirt, beauty and ugliness, and an opening out of the ordinary into the extraordinary,' writes Jay Griffiths. For my own part, they open up a space in which to host thoughts that I would otherwise find silly or ridiculous: that voiceless awe at the passing of time. The way everything changes. The way everything stays the same. The way those things are bigger than I am, and more than I can hold.

More than any other season, winter requires a kind of metronome that ticks away its darkest beats, giving us a melody to follow into spring. The year will move on either way, but by paying attention to it, feeling its beat, and noticing the moments of transition – perhaps even taking time to think about what we want from the next phase in the year – we can get the measure of it.

If we resist the instinct to endure those darkest moments alone, we might even make the opportunity to share the burden, and to let a little light in.

EPIPHANY

WHEN YOU START TUNING IN to winter, you realise that we live through a thousand winters in our lives – some big, some small. Just as I was coming to the end of H's illness and mine, and was beginning to believe that life was about to settle down again, I realised that a grand winter had rolled in without my even realising it.

My son had grown too anxious to go to school. Six years old, and he had been overpowered by it already: that toxic soup of thirty kids packed into one classroom, a teacher pulled in so many different directions that Bert felt invisible, and a couple of mean boys in the playground. A hyperactive curriculum that made him feel like he couldn't keep up; a set of blanket targets which meant that 'expected' was all we ever heard about him.

I knew about his worries; I had been listening. But I hadn't been hearing properly. The seriousness of the situation took me by surprise. I had thought that his problems were ordinary, and it turned out that they were not. I had offered soothing words, some small attempts at problem-solving, the reassurance that all the best people hate school. What he needed was a riot. What he needed was for me to rise up and say, 'You know what? This isn't good enough! My son deserves to be happy!'

Because he wasn't happy. I hadn't noticed the joy seeping out of him, but it had seeped all the same. Some winters are gradual. Some winters creep up on us so slowly that they have infiltrated every part of our lives before we truly feel them. His rage at school seemed sudden, but it was not. He had been telling me about it all along, and now he was making sure I'd heard.

So I finally let his words sink in. I pulled him out of school, and shrugged off suggestions for ways to shoehorn him back in again: how to threaten and cajole; how to charm him into tolerating it; whether I should medicate him into submission. I would do none of those things. I was not willing to get him back into school by breaking him, however desperate I was for my own time again. I, who had essentially liked the rhythm and challenge of school, came to realise how many people found school an utter endurance, but that many of them nevertheless believed that our children should endure it too, for fourteen painful years of their life. I was supposed to worry about his future qualifications more than his ability to be content. I was not willing to do that. I didn't feel that the two should be in conflict – achieving your potential, and not being completely miserable. Happiness is the greatest skill we'll ever learn; it is not a part of ourselves that should be hived off into a dark corner, the shameful territory of the wilfully naive.

Happiness *is* our potential, the product of a mind that's allowed to think as it needs to, that has enough of what it requires, that is free of the terrible weight of bullying and humiliation. As children, we tolerate working conditions that we'd find intolerable as adults: the constant interrogation of our attainment to a hostile audience, the motivation by threat instead of encouragement (and big threats, too: *if you don't do this, you'll ruin your whole future life* ...), the social world in which you're mocked and teased, your most embarrassing desires exposed, your new-formed body held up for the kind of scrutiny that would destroy an adult. Often, in childhood, this comes with physical threats, too – being pushed and shoved in the playground, punched and kicked. The eternal menace that something more savage is waiting around the corner on your way home. Imagine how that would feel to you now: that perpetual threat to your bodily integrity and your mental well-being. We would never stand for it, but we did as children because it was expected of us, and we didn't know any better.

But if happiness is a skill, then sadness is too. Perhaps through all those years at school, or perhaps through other terrors, we are taught to ignore it, to stuff it down into our satchels and pretend it isn't there. As adults, we often have to learn to hear the clarity of its call. That is wintering. It is the active acceptance of sadness. It is the practice of allowing ourselves to feel it as a need. It is the courage to stare down the worst parts of our experience, and to commit to healing them the best we can. Wintering is a moment of intuition, our true needs felt keenly as a knife.

The time had come to teach my son to winter. It's quite a skill to pass on. So we took our time and sank into the things we love: we played on the beach, and burrowed through the library. We made pirates out of air-drying clay, and walked in the woods to bring home pine cones and berries. We took the train up to London and visited the Natural History Museum to see the dinosaurs in relative solitude. One particularly cold morning, we took advantage of a hoar frost to make strangely indestructible snowballs. We baked cookies and kneaded pizza dough, and played more Minecraft than I would have liked.

We travelled through the dark moments together. I won't pretend it was fun but it was necessary all the time. We raged and grieved together. We were overcome with fear. We worried and slept it off, and didn't sleep, and let our timetables turn upside down. We didn't so much retreat from the world as let it recede from us. We howled out in pain to our friends and family, and were surprised that so many rushed in to assist us, sometimes with practical support, but sometimes just by sharing stories of their own. It helped. We felt broken into pieces, but at the same time, never so loved.

In our winter, a transformation happened. We read, and we worked, and we problem-solved, and we found new solutions. We changed our focus away from pushing through with normal life, and towards making a new one. When everything is broken, everything is also up for grabs. That's the gift of winter: it's irresistible. Change will happen in its wake, whether we like it or not. We can come out of it wearing a different coat.

The greatest wisdom came from people who had endured this particular winter before us. I met them first when I was sitting in a noisy trampolining centre on a Wednesday morning, feeling conspicuously like I was accompanying a child who ought to be in school. I was actually waiting for a tap on the shoulder, perhaps from the centre manager, perhaps from a lurking truancy officer, if indeed they still exist. But when a tap on the shoulder came, it was from a woman sitting in a group on a nearby table. 'Are you a home schooler too?' she said.

And I blurted out what felt like my entire life history, or at least everything that had gone wrong in the past few months. I expected them to be shocked at my incompetence as a mother, but instead my story was met with smiles and nods, sympathetic tilts of the head. 'I'd say everyone around this table has been through exactly the same thing,' she said.

I could have stood there and cried on the spot, just knowing that I wasn't alone.

I sat down with them and learned that my son was just one of hundreds of children across the county who felt flattened by school, and that I was one of hundreds of parents who felt a gut refusal to force him back into it and to train him to take the consequences. The parents told me how it took a while, but that their children had become happy again out of mainstream schooling, having been violently unhappy within it. 'She's a different child now,' said one. 'She's recovered a part of herself that we thought was lost forever.' I followed her gaze to watch a little girl whirling and skipping between the trampolines, a picture of freedom. And my own son, playing happily with another boy from the group.

'Look at them. They're like two peas in a pod,' she said. I felt accepted in a way that I hadn't for months.

Here is another truth about wintering: you'll find wisdom in your winter, and once it's over, it's your responsibility to pass it on. And in return, it's our responsibility to listen to those who have wintered before us. It's an exchange of gifts in which nobody loses out. This may involve the breaking of a lifelong habit, passed down carefully through generations: that of looking at other people's misfortunes and feeling certain that they brought them up upon themselves in a way that you never would. This isn't just an unkind attitude, it does us harm, because it stops us from learning that disaster happens, and how to adapt when it does. It stops us from reaching out to people who are suffering. And, when our own disaster comes, it forces us into a humiliated retreat, as we try to hunt down mistakes that we never made in the first place, or wrong-headed attitudes that we never held. Either that, or we become certain that there must be someone out there we can blame. Watching winter, and really listening to its messages, we learn that effect is often disproportionate to cause; that tiny mistakes can lead to huge disasters; that life is often bloody unfair, but it carries on happening with or without our consent. We learn to look kindly on other people's crises, because they are so often portents of our own future.

★

One night, I let Bert sit up late to finish watching the final Harry Potter film. We had started reading the books at the beginning of his troubles, and it quickly became clear that he identified with Harry, bullied and belittled, subject to flashes of temper, but also brave and loyal, a child who toughs out the bad times and relishes the good. Soon, we switched to the films just so that he could race through them faster. He'd got to the end of *The Deathly Hallows Part 1* and was so desolate that I had to show him how it all finished; had to prove to him that the tide would turn.

As the film starts, I take out a pencil and a piece of paper, and draw him the same diagram that I used to draw for my undergraduates: a curve on a graph, rather like a wonky smile.

'This is the shape of a good story,' I say. 'This is the beginning, and the end. And in the middle, see, is always the lowest point. It's called the nadir: the moment when things have got so bad that you just can't imagine a way out.'

Bert examines it for a while. 'So that's where we are,' he says, and points to the very bottom of the curve. 'Here.'

I am no longer sure which curve we're talking about: ours or Harry's, but I suppose they're both the same. 'Yes,' I say, and then I shift my pencil a little to the right. 'And the fightback begins *here.*'

'So after that it all gets better?'

'Not quite. There are ups and downs. But from now on, the hero of the story is working towards a solution. Even with each setback, he gains ground.'

Bert takes my pencil and draws over my line. He follows the original curve, but takes a series of deep dives along the way.

'So this is what it's really like,' he says. 'This is how stories work.'

'Yes,' I say. 'Except in real life, it carries on happening. The adventure doesn't end on the last page.'

★

I make a new ritual for the Christmas period this year, in those twelve days that I always struggle to fill meaningfully. It starts at the solstice and ends on New Year's Day.

At sunset after the solstice, I gather with some friends to light a fire on the beach, dragging my fire bowl and a bag of logs through the town in my old shopping trolley. It's unseasonably mild, so much so that I notice the cat moulting the next morning, as if she's done with winter and ready to move on.

Nevertheless, the wind gusts and blasts as I try to light the newspaper underneath my kindling, blowing out fifteen matches and making me mutter curses under my breath. I'm beginning to think we won't have a fire at all when someone arrives with a lighter, and makes my Girl Guide efforts look primitive. Soon, it's burning palely in the low, slanting sun, making our shadows long, and we stand on the shingle in our coats, clutching flasks of tea and mulled wine, drinking beer from bottles.

The tide is far out. Our children play at the edges of the beach, conspiring about the toys they will get, daring each other to believe in Father Christmas for just one more year. We watch the sun, which is putting on a golden display below scattered grey clouds, dipping ever closer to the horizon. Whitstable beach is a popular spot for watching sunsets; I bathe in any number of them in the summer. On those days, it dips into the sea to the right of the Isle of Sheppey. Today, at its furthest winter extent, it is over to the left, descending behind the low houses at Seasalter. I have long known that the sun moves across the sky over the course of the year, but I have never noticed it before. In winter, it makes an entirely different retreat, above marshland instead of sea.

We watch the last peak of its circle disappear, and then the fire seems to burn brighter. I find myself wishing we had a song to sing, a carol or a hymn to the return of the light. 'We have turned the year,' I say, as I learned to do at Stonehenge a mere few hours before. The phrase is repeated between our group, back and forth like an echo: we have turned the year.

We have turned the year.

We have turned the year.

It would have happened either way, with or without our noticing, but this way gives us the fleeting impression that we have seized control, not of the seasons, but of our response to them. The sky is now a thin blue, still light enough to see, but crisper and colder. The children stalk off to find the edge of the sea, and soon come back, covered in mud and entirely fed up of being out in the dark. Somebody takes them home to watch *Elf*, and we adults find ourselves in a quiet mood, each of us holding our own thoughts. We stoke the fire. A full moon rises above the town, looking for all the world as though it has popped up to take over where the sun left off. Soon, it is shining fiercely against a blackening sky.

The beach is empty except for us. We huddle closer to the fire, enjoying the quiet and burning the rest of the logs. When I used to live in a house overlooking the beach, I often watched people build enormous bonfires that blazed high into the air. My small metal bowl is far less ambitious, but it throws out a generous dose of heat. We mutter hopes that the next year might be easier. We repeat the phrase, *we have turned the year*, almost in wonder. At some point, the sea starts whispering from deep in the darkness, and we realise that the tide has turned, too.

The following morning, having failed to persuade anyone to return to the beach to watch the sun come back up again, I stand in the garden to do it alone. I have no clear line of sight to the horizon, so I can only clutch my mug of tea and notice the day ease in. At first, the stars are out, impossibly bright specks against a black sky. But then, the birds begin to stir in anticipation of the sun. The call of the herring gulls rises, and I begin to see their silhouettes above me, and realise that the stars have faded. The robin sings when the sky is nearly blue. And then, in the gap between two houses, there is golden light, and the world is bright again.

That day marks the beginning of Christmas for me. As befits the end of a crisis-prone year, I have left it late, but I spend the morning in the local grocers, bringing in the Christmas provisions: stilton, ham, Brussels sprouts, a capon of terrifying dimensions. Unfathomable quantities of potatoes. Red wine and white, a bottle of Marsala. Turkish delight and cherry liqueur chocolates. A bag of satsumas, some wrapped in blue and gold paper. Several pots of cream, just in case.

I do all of my present shopping, too, in one big hit. It feels more generous than a slow accumulation of gifts across several months: it's a spree, a joyful piling of boxes and packages into my basket, a dizzying handover of money at the till. As I have done since he was a baby, I buy Bert a fresh pair of pyjamas for Christmas Eve; this year's are pale blue with bicycles. I come home and feel ready, and not at all like I resisted Christmas until the last moment. Instead, I have addressed it in its place, and at the right time, making it a joy instead of a labour.

On Christmas Eve, we are obliged to lay on a buffet for Santa, or so it seems; Bert has thought of a whole list of refreshments that the great man might need (all of which must be labelled), and still more for his reindeer. This being done, we hang up Bert's stocking on the door handle, and notice at the last moment that he's booby-trapped it with a looped belt, in the hope that he will wake and catch a glimpse of Santa. I'm slyly proud of his ingenuity; less so later, when I'm untangling the thing after a couple of glasses of that Marsala. But padding downstairs to stuff a Christmas stocking is one of the high points of my year, a gesture of abundance and thoughtfulness. I love packing in the traditional items (gold coins and a chocolate orange in the toe for my fruit-refuser) and the clutch of knick-knacks, insignificant in themselves, but made special by the intimacy they represent, that knowledge of the silly little things that will make your child smile. I'd be tempted to resent Saint Nick for taking all the credit, if he didn't add so much magic.

On Christmas Day, we wrangle an avalanche of Lego, and eat, and drink, and throw a ball on the beach. On Boxing Day, we fry bubble and squeak, and bring out plates of leftovers and pickles for good friends. Then, we enter that strange period between Christmas and New Year, when time seems to muddle, and we keep finding ourselves asking, 'What day is it? What date?' I always mean to work on these days, or at least to write, but this year, like every other, I find myself unable to gather up the necessary intent. I used to think that these were wasted days, but I now realise that's the point. I am doing nothing very much, not even actively being on holiday. I clear out my cupboards, ready for another year's onslaught of cooking and eating. I take Bert out to play with friends. I go for cold walks that make my ears ache. I am not being lazy; I'm not slacking; I'm just letting my attention shift for a while, away from the direct ambitions of the rest of my year. It's like revving my engines.

On New Year's Eve, I feel the familiar dread; the pressure of the party season in its final gasp. I don't think I've ever managed to party out the New Year effectively; perhaps once, very long ago. My family used to stage a cut-down Christmas lunch on New Year's Day, a good idea that we've abandoned. Nowadays, I don't make any plans at all, and then regret it when the evening arrives. I always think I should at least have cooked dinner for a few good friends. But the politics of New Year seem excessively complicated to me. Even at the ripe old age of forty-one, I'm shy of asking if anyone's free, lest I make myself look unpopular. Then, every year without fail, I discover the next day that many of my favourite people were sitting at home, bored, and brooding on the same dark thoughts that I was: *I bet everyone else is out there having fun. Why wasn't I invited?*

Children complicate New Year, of course. It's probably mean to say that they ruin the fun, but they certainly present a quandary: let them stay up, and you'll spend a whole evening negotiating with small people in varying states of grouchiness and over-excitement; pack them off to bed, and you'll be haunted by the sense that you've excluded them from a key moment of celebration. For my own part, I promise Bert that he can stay up, and that we'll go out on to the beach at midnight to watch the fireworks that are spontaneously let off all along the coast every year. But at 8.30pm, it's clear he's already flagging, and so I strike a complex deal involving an immediate bonfire and then bed, providing we all keep up the pretence that it's actually midnight.

He reluctantly agrees, and we burn the Christmas tree (stripped and chopped up earlier) while sipping cheap champagne. It's actually a brilliant end to the season, if a little earlier than I would have preferred: the tree is so dry from a month indoors that the needles crackle each time we throw a branch on the fire. We watch them glow bronze and then disintegrate into the flames, and then repeat until the whole tree is nothing but a pile of ashes. Afterwards, I lie down with him while he drifts resentfully off to sleep, and then creep downstairs to drink a final martini and to watch *Hootenanny* on TV, ever the signal of a wasted New Year. Next year, I say, we'll make proper plans. H laughs at me.

This, then, is how I turned my year: not in a single, high-stakes moment, but in a series of gestures that gently acknowledge the change taking place, but which have an eye on the continuities, too. It's the twelve days of Christmas, but shifted a little. There are no diets in the days that follow, no pledges to go vegan or dry. I have nothing for which to atone. But, for the first time in my life, the boundary between December and January begins to feel a little less arbitrary, linked to the return of the light, and the promise of spring. No doubt, the winter will still have plenty of remaining bite; the coldest days are yet to come, and, if we follow last year's pattern, we have at least two months to wait until we can expect any snow. But there will be snowdrops soon, and then the first crocuses. It won't be long. The year begins again.

JANUARY

DARKNESS

I HAVE ONLY EVER CROSSED the Arctic Circle once. I was five months pregnant, anaemic, woozy with high blood pressure and sick as a dog. It was probably not the best idea I'd ever had, but then I had booked the trip a long time in advance, before I'd even thought I could get pregnant at all.

Motherhood came to me earlier than I'd expected. Approaching my mid-thirties, I had become alarmed at a cluster of magazine articles telling me that I was almost certainly dicing with my future fertility, but I was also gripped by the notion that I needed to get an awful lot better at being an adult before I could produce a child. As I have for most of my life, I felt that I was just on the cusp of getting it all right, and only needed a little more time. My solution was a characteristically icy one: I decided to freeze some of my eggs until that unspecified later date when I would have figured it all out.

On a day so rainy that I was wet to my underwear by the time I arrived, I attended a fertility clinic near London Bridge for a range of tests aimed at taking an exact snapshot of my fertility. I was hoping to join a scheme that allowed me to harvest and freeze my eggs for free, in return for donating some of the spare ones which, after all, were sitting around unused. But the results were not what I expected. Rather than telling me how much time I had left, the tests told me that I had no time left at all. I had plenty of eggs, but I wasn't producing the right hormones to get pregnant. I was kidding myself that I was in any kind of control.

I limped home that night, sending out a barrage of perky texts to the effect that I was *so* glad that I'd found this out, and that information is the best armour, and I could now make informed decisions; that I was lucky to *know*, in a way that so many women never do; that – ha, ha – I now regretted all those years spent messing about with contraceptives. If only I'd found out sooner! Funny really. When you came to think of it. And then I got into bed, pulled the covers over my head, and cried.

Until that point, I'd had the luxury of ambivalence; of thinking that I could have a child or maybe not, depending on how my life went. I could see a good life either way. But now, the certainty hit me like a hammer blow: I wanted a child. I had always wanted a child. I just hadn't had the guts to admit it until that moment.

Within a week, I was signed up to a different kind of fertility clinic: an NHS one, geared towards IVF. In the four months it took to get the first appointment, our lives changed completely. Having read every book I could get my hands on, I had bought a jumbo bag of ovulation detectors on eBay, and was now peeing on a stick every morning, examining my cervical mucous and recording my temperature on a spreadsheet. We were having the kind of conception sex that sounds like it might be fun, but which quickly becomes unbearably tedious. All of this was highly unlikely to work, but at least I felt like I was making a contribution. I was also visiting an acupuncturist, just in case it happened to be effective. My lifelong suspicion of alternative medicine no longer mattered. I was throwing everything I had at the problem, scattergun.

I'll never be sure what worked or what didn't, but I turned up pregnant to my first IVF appointment. They took me straight in for a scan, and I saw a tiny, twitching cluster of cells, its heart not yet really a heart, but nevertheless beating. It was beyond unexpected, and years earlier than I'd planned, and I was completely terrified, but also desperate to cling on to this strange form of life inside me.

Miserably ill for the whole first trimester, I considered cancelling my trip to Tromsø, but couldn't quite bear the thought. I told myself that it would fall in the golden second trimester, when everyone assured me I'd feel invincible. That moment never really came. In fact, I just seemed to accumulate more niggling complications and impediments. But I couldn't let go of the idea of travelling north. In fact, it became the point against which I marked off the grim, restricted weeks. I very nearly clung to the idea to get me through.

As the time grew closer, my midwife expressed her doubts as to whether I should go. I have never been fond of asking permission, but in this case I needed her to sign a letter declaring me safe to travel, lest I invalidate my insurance. I was also slightly worried that the airline would refuse to take me: I was already the size of a whale and I thought they might suspect me of carrying a full-term Jonah. The letter, I felt, would prevent me from getting stranded in an airport.

She kept me waiting for her final decision, refusing to call it too early. I told her that she had to let me go; I had an urge to see the northern lights, and it couldn't be defeated. She looked at me as though this was perhaps another new symptom that she ought to be concerned about, and let it be known that she was prevaricating for my own good. But I think she also understood. I could feel a change coming, and this was the last gasp of my adult independence rearing up. She finally agreed four days before we were due to fly, on the proviso that there was sufficient disaster-planning in place. I showed her the distance between our hotel and the hospital, and promised that I could sit and watch TV all day if need be. It was grimly agreed that the Norwegians could be trusted with maternity care, should the worst happen.

It was a strange destination for a last hurrah. We finally flew out in late January, with everything thoroughly frozen and dark. I struggled to find any kind of warm coat that would also fit around my bump, and soon discovered the brutal bodily processes that prioritised the blood flow to my uterus when the temperature dropped below zero, often leaving me juddering with cold. I found the food unbearably salty, and tinned pineapple – my sole pregnancy craving – in short supply. The Norwegian prices were alarmingly high anyway, so we mostly ate in our room, improvising meals from pasta and the few fresh vegetables we could find. We did make a couple of trips to the local Burger King, which boasted proudly of being the northernmost example of its kind. But that was guilt-inducing, especially with my blood pressure. Tromsø felt more like the last outpost of civilisation than the 'Paris of the North'. It was exactly what I needed.

From the end of November until the middle of January, Tromsø experiences the polar night, when the sun doesn't rise at all. Because the earth's axis is tilted, there are around forty days in the year when it is permanently facing away from the sun. This doesn't mean that it's plunged into complete darkness; instead, there is a short daytime period in which the light is a kind of navy blue, like the first moments after sunset. This may not seem like a lot, but for those who live through it, it marks a vital distinction between day and night. For Tromsø, the reign of the polar night lasts a little longer than it naturally would, because the surrounding mountains block any view of the rising sun for an extra week. When we arrived, the sun had only just made its first appearance, and that was brief. The night seemed to last from around three in the afternoon until about nine in the morning. Then there was an extended period of dawn, with the briefest of days in the middle, before twilight began again.

I wasn't there for long enough to adapt to it; instead, I found myself sleeping for most of each day, lulled by the endless midwinter beige. It was easy to sleep in all that darkness, and, honestly, it made a pleasant change from feeling exhausted all the time. When I was awake, I was mainly worrying about slipping on the pavements, or vomiting in public, or straying too far from the University Hospital of North Norway, which became my lodestar. Winter sports were certainly off the itinerary, and no tour operator would let me near huskies, which were apparently renowned for their love of rough-and-tumble. I felt as though I had been intrepid in all the wrong ways: I had overreached, overcompensated for my fears that this would mark an end to my freedom. But there was magic everywhere: extraordinary ice escarpments at the sides of the roads, and babies sleeping in prams piled with quilts, like the pea in the princess's bed. And each night, my regrets dissipated as we hunted for the aurora borealis, the famed northern lights that were at one of the cyclical peaks in their activity.

On the first evening, we boarded a fishing boat that sailed out of Tromsø harbour, and fed us with freshly caught cod in the cosy cabin, with all the other tourists comparing husky sledding injuries. We had barely finished our meal when we were called onto deck because the skipper thought he'd seen something, and as we watched, a wisp of greenish smoke appeared overhead, almost close enough to touch. Untutored, I would have assumed it was a stray emission from one of the surrounding boats, but this, apparently, was the aurora: pale, evanescent, but tangible in a way that I hadn't expected. It wasn't an image flashed across the sky; it was actually there, an object in three dimensions, drifting slowly above our boat.

It was our first encounter, and the most doubtful. After that moment, I realised that every image of the lights I had ever seen had been misleading. I had been poring over photographs of neon displays as lurid as disco lights, and watching YouTube videos of lights that strike out against the night sky, bold and distinct. These are invariably sped up, the luminous greens and pinks enhanced by long exposures. Look closely, and you will see the stars shining through the aurora in every picture; they are not even bright enough to eclipse tiny pinpoints of light from trillions of miles away. They move slowly, like drifting clouds. Seeing them is an uncertain experience, almost an act of faith. You have to get your eye in, and I honestly don't think I would ever have spotted them at all had I not been told they were there.

There is nothing showy about the northern lights, nothing obvious or demanding. They hide from you at first, and then they whisper to you. We would squint into the sky, and say, 'Is that them, there? Do you think? Over there? Yes. Yes! Maybe. I don't know …' But then, eventually, at a pace set entirely by the firmament, we were given the gift of seeing them, as if in reward for our faith and patience. Then, we seemed to see them everywhere.

I must have watched hundreds of videos on the aurorae by now, and read dozens of articles, and I still feel only on a knife-edge of understanding what they are. They result from a collision of forces of which I was barely aware before I planned my visit to Tromsø. The earth has a magnetic force, and charged particles – protons and electrons – in the magnetospheric plasma that surrounds us are blown into the upper atmosphere by solar winds. Here, they ionise, emitting light and colour. It's a process that I think I understand while writing it down, but which I know from experience that I will immediately forget as soon as I step away from my laptop. The speed and acceleration of the particles, the latitude at which the collisions take place and the presence of other elements all affect the display – red, green, yellow and blue are all possible, but green is the most common. They are mostly only visible against dark skies, in areas of low light pollution.

I could have walked away after that first night, satisfied that I had seen what I came all that way to see, but I had the sense that more was to come. So on the second night, we set out by coach at 10pm and drove for miles along roads with icy banks at either side. Our tour guides twitched endlessly on mobile phones to keep up with the latest sightings, and several times the coach driver performed a precarious U-turn and headed off in a different direction to pursue a tip-off. Every hour or so, we would park up and be issued with matching orange hi-vis vests, before filing out and gazing hopefully into the sky. It didn't always pay off. But eventually I found myself standing on a frozen shore, watching an enormous green eye form in the sky above me, and then dissipate. It was every bit as indistinct as the previous night's sighting, but alive somehow, and crackling at the edge of my hearing. Blink and you lost it. Point an iPhone camera at it, and it grew shy again. But the guides had SLR cameras and tripods, and we all came home with a grinning photograph of ourselves under intense green light, which we never could have perceived through our own eyes.

That night, at 2am, we got out at a forest clearing, and our guide joked, 'There are bears in these woods, but don't worry, they've never eaten anyone yet!' Then he looked at me for a few beats. 'I wonder if pregnant women send out different pheromones, though.' At that moment, I realised that I was shuddering so hard with cold that my arms were jerking beside me, and also that I was pretty close to vomiting all over that pristine snow. If my pheromones didn't attract the bears, then perhaps that would. I retreated back to the bus, and slept off the rest of the night's expedition, dreaming of those slow emerald drifts of light.

I could certainly have given up the next day, and considered myself satisfied. But by then I was almost addicted, feeling compelled to get my lifetime's worth of ionising plasma while I still had the chance. We caught a bus north and boarded a red ship that churned south again through the fjords. Standing on its deck, I watched a pinkish fringe of light that rippled just above my head, as if the wind had caught the curtain at an open window. There seemed to be so many wonderful permutations of the aurorae, but all of them were fleeting, as if the line between your hopes and the reality was unclear. It was an experience not dissimilar from pregnancy itself: the sense, one moment, that something very definite is there, and the realisation, the next, that everything you know about it is a daydream.

At the end of the holiday, dropping into a hotel lobby in search of my lost mittens, I spotted the faint glow of the aurora just above the harbour, and supposed it might have been there all along, just waiting for me to learn how to see it.

★

We didn't only roam around in the night. One morning, we took a minibus out to Whale Island to meet a Sámi family and their reindeer. The drive took us through the snowy Lyngen Alps, behind which the sun was rising, staining the mountains rose pink. We passed fjords where people were swimming despite the unthinkable cold, and I began to absorb the connection between beauty and hardiness that existed in this freezing place; the way that these people worked hard to maintain their contract with the sublime.

Once we'd arrived, we were kitted out in snowsuits and enormous Davy Crockett hats, which we were told to put on over the top of anything we were already wearing. Then we were taken into a *lavvu* – a traditional temporary Sámi dwelling, arranged in a circle rather like a tipi – where we sat around a fire and contemplated just how cold it was. Given that I'd struggled to find a snowsuit baggy enough to fit, everyone in the group became aware that I was pregnant, and I suddenly gained an uncomfortable level of celebrity. The women in our party fussed and tutted around me, and wondered aloud why on earth I'd come all the way out here in this condition. Sitting down is the same anywhere in the world, I joked, weakly. I was warned, for at least the nineteenth time that week, to steer well clear of any huskies, and asked for probably the hundredth time whether I was watching *One Born Every Minute*. I was, but said I was not, hoping to prevent the group therapy session on childbirth that always seemed to follow. I achieved nothing of the sort, and was grateful to be let out eventually to meet the reindeer.

The Sámi are a people whose territory extends across the north of the peninsula where Norway, Sweden, Finland and Russia now join, although they have continuously inhabited it for close to ten millennia. As nation states began to form around them, the Sámi have often suffered from discrimination at the hands of the successive governments that arrived along the way, including being asked to prove ownership of the lands on which they have subsisted since time immemorial. Huge inequalities still exist, but they are now recognised as an indigenous people by Sweden, Norway and Finland, with their own devolved parliaments; in Russia, no such protections have been afforded and, as they have been for a long time now, the Sámi remain vulnerable to forced relocation and incursions into their territory. Theirs will always be a fragile position: a culture made up of a group of diverse cultures, living in a land within a group of diverse lands, seeking to retain a way of life that would horrify most contemporary Europeans.

The Sámi have traditionally survived by hunting, fishing, fur-trapping and the reindeer herding for which they are best known. Reindeer are entwined with their culture to the extent that, under Norwegian law, Sámi have an exclusive right to own the animals. They are used for food, for transport and clothing, and were even once accepted as currency in lieu of monetary taxation. Sámi herdsmen make a series of small cuts in the ears of their reindeer, known as 'earmarks', with each family having its own unique pattern. They are renowned for their intimate understanding of their herds and their life cycles.

Theirs is an animistic faith, based on the idea that souls can reside in a range of things: animals, plants and landscape features are often prominent subjects for animism. For the Sámi, this includes bears, ravens, seals, water, winds and *sieidis*, prominent rock formations that stand out in the surrounding landscape. A range of gods and spirits are shown fealty, ancestors are present in everyday life, and certain locations are honoured as significant to individual families. Unsurprisingly, reindeer loom large in the Sámi imagination. Beivve, the sun goddess, was thought to travel across the sky each day in a ring of reindeer antlers, casting fertility back down to earth. At the winter solstice, she received the sacrifice of a white female reindeer; as the sun began to return, she was offered gifts of butter, which were smeared onto doors to melt in her presence. Meanwhile, mythology tells of the Meandash, or reindeer people, born of a shaman woman who could change shape between human and reindeer. She was so wise and so ancient that, like the reindeer, she is thought to have existed before time.

My own expectations of the reindeer were considerably less sophisticated, hinging entirely on what I'd gleaned from a lifetime of Santa Claus. Up close, they were wilder than I'd hoped, with erratic flicks of the head, and eyes that roved in their sockets when we approached them, showing their whites. Some of them had mossy fur dangling from their antlers in shreds. 'That's because they're due to fall off soon, before the spring comes,' said Trine, our host. Reindeer bulls, she explained, use their antlers to fight over the females, shedding them at the end of the mating season when winter comes. They soon grow another set, but these are soft and tender for a few months, with blood vessels near the surface, and they aren't fully hardened until the autumn, when the animals start fighting all over again. The females, or cows, shed their antlers in a different cycle. They have their young just when the males' antlers are at their softest, so they keep their own antlers for longer to defend their calves against predators. That means that the ragged-antlered deer were all female, wearing their resilience like a crown.

Later, we each rode in a sleigh pulled by one of them – my own reindeer was carefully selected for its docility, but it was still a bumpy ride over the snow and around a frozen lake, all the while sitting on reindeer skins. Afterwards, we retired to the *lavvu* for some reindeer soup to strike back against the cold. As

I finished my bowl, Trine hurried over to replenish it. 'You do not have your antlers, Mama Reindeer,' she said, 'so we must fill you up with soup instead.' I brimmed with tears, because she'd summed up something that I couldn't articulate until now: pregnancy made me feel as though I was missing some defence or other, and I couldn't fight for myself. The reindeer understood what was necessary to get through winter. I did not.

In Tromsø, I learned that extraordinary things can flourish in the dark, cold polar night, but I also realised that, no matter how hard I tried to fight it, I simply had no defence against the changes that were happening in my life. I was missing my antlers. I had skittered over to a different country to convince myself that I could carry on just as normal, but instead I only saw my own desperation, mirrored in the ice.

But it was there, too, that I came to a kind of acceptance: of my own limitations, and of the future that lay before me. I learned that I was not invincible at this moment in my life, but also that it wouldn't last forever. I learned to rest and to surrender. I learned to dream. I took photographs that I imagined showing to some future person, as yet unknown to me, and saying, *Look, here you are under the northern lights.*

Few of us inherit the rich and complex mythologies that the Sámi pass on – the sense of the world being alive around us, and of ancestors keeping a gentle watch residing in the very rocks we stand on, the very wind that buffets us. Most of us have to make our own, if we think to do it at all. In my time under the aurorae, I thought of the first gift of mythology that I could pass on to my son, the seed of his own personal lore. *You, who were so strong that I sometimes thought you'd overcome me entirely, crossed the Arctic Circle before you were even born ...*

Before we left, we chose the first toy that we'd dared to buy for him, a small, plush polar bear, soft and white, standing on all four feet. He's still called Tromsø.

HUNGER

I WALK IN THE LATE January frost, and I realise that I am a wolf today. I had already been overcome by the need to prowl: to go outside and stalk about my territory, restless and wary. There is an unrest in my gut that feels like hunger.

The sun is low, making gold streaks in the desiccated grasses that line my path. I am alert to birds, to the sudden bustle of movement in the bare red brambles. My mouth craves, and I cannot tell what it would make me do if I didn't stalk. Never having been a smoker in my life, I am craving a cigarette, just for the sense of occupation it would lend to my tongue and my lips; just for the feeling of transgression. Otherwise, I think it would be a drink, at this time in the morning. My mouth wants it. It wants the disruption of a long, intent swallow, and the daze it might bring. I suddenly see why cigarettes are a lesser evil in those dark, disrupted moments, when the mouth will use anything to avoid crying out its pain.

Instead, I walk. I have learned to walk at these moments. I have learned to walk until the heat goes out of it.

★

I once met a man who tracked wolves. He turned up at the launch party for an anthology I'd edited, a friend of a friend. I quickly lost interest in anything else that was going on in the room; all my carefully nurtured authors had to fend for themselves. The wolf man was the only game in town.

There was a quality about him – a stark, intent gaze – that I found utterly captivating. He had no artifice; no social nicety. Instead, he had something wild, elemental. It's hard to put into words without sounding like an over-boiled romance novel, particularly when, later that evening, you are attempting to explain your fascination with this man to your slightly startled husband. But my interest wasn't romantic; it was more like the call of the wild. It seemed to me that he was part-wolf, and that, in his time living on the trail of those creatures that he clearly adored, he had absorbed some of their essence.

He told me that he began his lupine career as an itinerant shepherd in the Greek mountains, trying to escape the pressure to get a proper job. As he was an Englishman, wolves had never featured much in his imagination, but here they were an ever-present threat, a predator for which he had to be continually watchful. He learned that wolves often kill more than they can eat, which leads to a reputation for killing for sport; on discovering an unattended flock of sheep, a wolf pack will likely slay the lot of them, rather than simply snatch one or two. Wolves could certainly be cruel on occasion, but what struck him with far more force was the cruelty of humans towards wolves.

Our fear of them – instinctive, ancestral – led to a thirst for wolf blood that far exceeded the threat of the wolves towards us. The surrounding farmers in the Greek hills hated the wolves, and wanted them dead. Bearing in mind that the sheep had an uncanny knack of shortening their own lives by straying into rivers or off the sides of escarpments, the impact of the wolves' hunger, it seemed, was minimal. But the fear of them wasn't rational, he told me. If you pushed the farmers for an explanation, the argument always came down to this: sheep are one thing, but give wolves an inch and they'll soon be snatching children. It was hard to find evidence of this ever happening, but it was always enough of a reason for a cull.

My friend started to pay more attention to wolves than to sheep. He began to observe them, studying their behaviour and habits, becoming intimate with the nearby pack, so that he felt as if he knew each one as an individual. He developed strategies to better protect sheep from wolves, and started to advise other nearby landowners on how to avoid wolf attacks in ways that were more effective and less costly than a cull. 'They thought I was mad,' he said, 'but they knew I was right.'

He was no longer a shepherd, but now a wolf consultant, travelling across Europe to catch the scent of scattered populations of *Canis lupus*. Sometimes he was called in to find out if populations still existed at all in certain regions; other times, he was asked to assess the size and strength of a pack, and to advise on their conservation. He said that he learned to live like the wolves, to think like them, to merge into their landscape just as they did. Years of existing alone in forests, stalking one of the great predators, had heightened his senses to the point that human society felt unbearable. Without a doubt, he had taken on their traits, but to be wolf-like for him was to be quiet and watchful, intent, pared back. As he spoke, his gaze was always steady, frank. Next to him, I felt like an entirely frivolous being, all cultivation and artifice. I was a domestic pet, and he a wild animal. A certain raw edge had been bred out of me.

What he came to believe, from all his wanderings across the continent, was that one thing was consistent in the lives of wolves: wherever they lived, they were subject to genocide. We talk as though wolf populations are dying out, he told me, but they're actually being systematically and brutally killed. Even where they're a protected species, the authorities politely look away as they're trapped and shot, poisoned and beaten. A wolf's death is often handled with superstitious ritual, subject to an excessive thoroughness that suggests a belief that wolves have supernatural powers. They are in fact the opposite, he told me. They are sensitive animals, exuding delicate emotion; magnificent parents; devoted children. They only attack livestock in extreme desperation. And if we eradicate them altogether, then where does that leave us? The wolf is a part of our collective psyche, as elemental to our thinking as the sun and the moon.

January's full moon was traditionally called the Wolf Moon, commemorating the time when wolves were most likely to be driven out of forests and into villages by hunger. It also marked the beginning of the medieval wolf-hunting season, when cubs were young, so that wolf packs were more vulnerable, and high-quality fur was on offer. There are records of the Anglo-Saxon kings demanding annual tributes in wolf skins from key landowners, or criminals being required to pay their debt to society in a certain quantity of wolf tongues. Some villages dug deep wolf pits to trap them; the Suffolk village of Woolpit derives its name from its own *wulf pytt*. Meanwhile, in Anglo-Saxon law, an outlaw was known as a *wulfheafod* or wolf's head, because he could be killed by anyone without fear of retribution. This was an echo of an earlier practice of tying a severed wolf's head around the neck of a convicted criminal, and driving him into the wilderness. Turning man into wolf was the ultimate debasement; a way of signalling a total loss of humanity and the rights that came with it.

The hunting of wolves was never discouraged under the Norman kings, but Edward I, who reigned from 1272 to 1307, was the first king to formally order the extermination of all wolves in England. For his own part, he employed one Peter Corbet, a wolf hunter, and tasked him with ensuring the death of all the wolves in Gloucestershire, Herefordshire, Worcestershire, Shropshire and Staffordshire. The areas around the Welsh Marches were seen as particularly dangerous. The wolves fought on, but by 1509, at the end of Henry VII's reign, they were thought to be extinct in England, or at least so rare as to pose no threat. Their elimination in Scotland seems to have come nearly two centuries later, with the last wolf reportedly being killed in 1680; however, sightings were reported as late as 1888. With their uncanny ability to melt into woodland, it is always difficult to say whether a wolf is there or not.

But wolves *are* still there. There are an estimated 12,000 of them in Europe (300,000 across the world), and their numbers are rising. Whether we see them or not, they continue to haunt our collective imagination, a symbol of low cunning and the rapacious hunger of winter. They endure as a reminder of the wild potential of the lands outside our busy, well-lit towns and cities; of the capacity of nature to still be red in tooth and claw. They are the ultimate fairy-tale villain, cropping up wherever there is a vulnerable creature to be devoured, be it a little pig or a grandmother.

They are everywhere in the literature of winter. In John Masefield's novel *The Box of Delights*, the wolves are running, representing an ancient force that menaces all the good magic in the world. In C. S. Lewis's Narnia, they are allies of the White Witch, treacherous, vicious creatures, driven towards the service of evil by a pack mentality. Meanwhile, in Joan Aiken's alternative history *The Wolves of Willoughby Chase*, the wolves are an incursion of the wild North into rural England, having migrated through the Channel Tunnel to escape the bitter cold of Russia. They represent an ever-present menace lurking just beyond the gates of civilised society, threatening travellers and straying children. And in *Game of Thrones*, a litter of direwolf pups appears at the start of the sequence, and quickly becomes a harbinger of the oft-threatened winter that haunts all the characters.

Wherever we want to denote the hunger of the cold season, we turn to wolves. They are the enemy we love to hate, offering us a glimpse of feral intelligence. Their morality is mutable. They do what they have to do. In the wolf, we are offered a mirror of ourselves as we might be, without the comforts and constraints of civilisation.

★

In the depths of our winters, we are all wolfish: we want in the archaic sense of the word, as if we are lacking something and need to absorb it in order to be whole again. These wants are often astonishingly inaccurate: drugs and alcohol that poison instead of reintegrate; relationships with people who do not make us feel safe or loved; objects that we do not need and cannot afford, and which hang around our necks like albatrosses of debt long after the yearning for them has passed. For some of us, this doesn't signify much in the long term: we flourish again and pay off those debts, or someone steps in for us. But for others, the excesses of the dark times cast a long shadow that is not so easily dispelled.

'I have never, ever been good with money,' says Marianne, 'and it's not like I come from a family who are bad with money. I was clueless.' In 2015, Marianne finally paid off an enormous credit card debt that had accumulated over the course of her adult life and which at one point threatened to engulf her. She had mostly done this the hard way, cutting back on anything but the essentials, and chipping away at the sum year by year, month by month until it was gone. Hers is not a story of wild excess, but of the accumulation of ordinary things.

'I left university debt-free,' she tells me, 'but then I went to work full-time and met the ex-husband.' He was, she says, 'financially incontinent. He had a taste for the finer things in life, but not the money to pay for it.' At the age of twenty-two, she took out her first credit card, and used it to buy her own engagement ring. It seemed practical at the time, but when she was offered a second card on the account, she made the mistake of getting one for her partner. After all, they were husband and wife. In the five years they were together, they racked up £15,000 of debt on that card, which is unexceptional. But then they split up, and two weeks after that, bailiffs appeared at Marianne's door to repossess the car. Soon after, a letter from the estate agents told her that she was to be evicted because her husband hadn't been paying the rent. At about this time, she realised that the credit card was in her name, so all the debt was hers.

At this point, she moved back in with her parents, and was still servicing the repayments without too much trouble. But the divorce added more debt to the pile, and although her ex was ordered to pay court costs, he didn't, and Marianne had to take him back to court. It took four years. 'I was unhappy,' she says, 'and I took the view that I deserved nice things, and that buying them would make me happier.'

By now, she had three or four credit cards, and although she kept taking out loans to pay them off, she would quickly build up the debt all over again. She was earning decent money, anyway. 'I don't remember the debt ever being higher than my salary,' she says, 'but I was in denial. I never sat down and added it all up.'

Then she moved job, and immediately regretted it. 'I absolutely hated it. I got seriously depressed and work-phobic. I couldn't contemplate even going there. There was a point when I realised that I was so stressed that carrying on would kill me, but that if I left, I couldn't service that debt.' By then, it stood at £38,000. 'I chose to leave and go bankrupt,' she says.

'I'd spent all this money thinking that it would make me happier, and here I was, no happier than before. It was an important lesson: I wasn't the stuff I'd bought. I'd wanted it to give me some kind of status. I haven't lived a very big life, and I was trying to buy the life I aspired to.'

Marianne's story has a bittersweet ending. She put her head down and gradually chipped away at her debt, and was able to pay it off after three years, following an unexpected windfall. But the years of worry have taken their toll on her mental health, and now, after several missteps and a redundancy, she has accepted a pay cut to get a simpler job, which is as much as she can cope with. 'I'm now living on the kind of money I had when I was paying off those debts,' she says, 'but with no end in sight.'

★

Life never does quite offer us those simple happy endings. I often think that it's all part of my own craving: the moral clarity of cause and effect, reward and punishment for my actions. A map for living that renders everything explicable. Instead, I am often left with the sense that my best acts are invisible, and that my worst are only revealed to me years after the event, when it's too late to atone.

Marianne may not be able to see immediate relief in her future, but to me, she has achieved something extraordinary, which is to be able to talk about her wolfish leanings without feeling shame. And nor should she. All her desires were for elemental things: love, a little comfort, the society of interesting people. Everyday life is so often isolated, dreary and lonely. A little craving is understandable. A little craving might actually be the rallying cry of survival.

In *Of Wolves and Men*, Barry Lopez examines the mystery of why wolves seem to kill more than they can eat. 'Wolves', he says, 'do not get hungry in the way we normally understand hunger. Their feeding habits and digestive systems are adapted to a feast-or-famine existence, and to procuring and processing massive amounts of food in a relatively short time. They are more or less always hungry.' They cannot tell when they will find their next meal, and they must ensure that their cubs and dependents have all they need, so they will kill any prey that presents itself as at a disadvantage. Failure to do this could mean starvation at an unspecified future point. The only place we routinely see an echo of this, he says, is in human hunters, who will often take all available prey, regardless of need.

Perhaps the wolf is such an enduring motif of hunger because we see in them a reflection of our own selves in lean times. In winter, those hungers become especially fierce. Like my fleeting friend, the wolf tracker, we should learn to respect our wolves. After all, despite centuries of human effort, they still endure, quietly surviving.

FEBRUARY

SNOW

I HAVE OFTEN HEARD TALK of the nostalgia of snow, the way that we always imagine our childhoods to be snowier than they actually were. Since my son was born, I have finally had a yardstick to measure it, and I can say with great certainty that we didn't have anything more than a smattering for the first six years of his life. We waited for it, impatient as children ourselves; every year, we would buy him a pair of warm padded trousers with a matching jacket at the beginning of the winter months, and every year they have hung on the coat rack, forlorn. Bert himself talks of snow as a kind of mythological beast, like the dragons he would wish into existence if he could.

I know for sure that I have never seen a white Christmas, but I do remember winters – more than one, I'm certain – when our village got cut off in the snow, with the electricity faltering and supplies in the local store dwindling. My mother came home with tales of an old woman snatching at the bread as if we'd all starve. People stood on their front door-steps to watch when the milk cart finally made it through.

In the winter of 1987, we had such deep snow that the drifts at the side of my school's lane towered above the car. Those of us who made it in were given soup at break-time to keep us warm – a choice of oxtail or tomato, served in an orange plastic beaker. I was allowed to wear a white roll-neck sweater under-neath my shirt and tie, and my mother let me wear my moon boots, saying that she would back me up if the teachers complained. At home, our house grew icicles so long and thick that we took to documenting them, measuring them with the sewing tape (one, I think, was four feet), and snapping them off to photograph them in the bath. Our house had no central heating, so all my snow-wet clothes had to be dried in front of the gas fire in the back room, and we worried that the Calor Gas heater would sputter out before the thaw. I can't say I minded. I was enthralled by the severity of our winter, its astonishing powers of change. I wanted it never to end.

I still retain a little of that attitude towards the snow. Try as I might, I can't effect the adult hardness towards a snowfall, full of resentment at the inconvenience. I

love the inconvenience the same way that I can sneak-
ingly love a bad cold: the irresistible disruption to
mundane life, forcing you to stop for a while and step
outside of your normal habits. I love the visual transformation that it brings about, that recolouring of the
world into sparkling white, and the way that the rules
change so that everybody says hello as they pass. I love
what it does to the light, the purplish clouds that loom
before it descends, and the way that it announces itself
from behind your curtains in the morning, glowing
with a diffuse whiteness that can only mean snow. I
love the feeling of it fresh underfoot, and heading out
in a snowstorm to catch it on my gloves. I am rarely
childlike and playful, except in snow. It swings me into
reverse gear.

Snow has that quality of awe in the sense of a power
greater than we are; it epitomises the aesthetic notion
of the sublime, in which greatness and beauty come
coupled with the power to overcome you entirely, as
a small, frail human.

I met with snow all through my adult life until I
had a child. I met it one year driving a chest of drawers
to the municipal dump, which was fine until I tried to
brake at the intersection with the main road and slid
right on across two lanes, slow and stately as a cruise
liner. Thankfully there were no other cars on the
road. I met it on the Eurostar to Paris, when it froze

the lines and stranded us well into the next week, and we were obliged to shrug and spend more time sitting in elegant cafes. I met it when I first moved to Whitstable, and found myself running onto an empty beach just to see what the sea looked like, crashing onto snow.

But Bert has been a kind of mascot against snow. I have a photograph of him as a baby, strapped to my front and wearing an ear-flapped hat as I walk through a scant two centimetres, but of course he doesn't remember that. I bought him a sledge as soon as he could walk, reasoning that if I left it until the snow actually came, the whole town would have sold out and we would end up on tea trays. It went unused, and ended up smashed in the back of the shed after we stacked other things on top of it. In Whitstable, with its warm microclimate, a sledge is a white elephant. I have even occasionally been tempted to drive him to witness a snowfall in a nearby town, or even a neighbouring county, but I'm fairly certain that blizzard tourism counts as parental irresponsibility.

Last winter he finally got his snow. There was a false start one Sunday morning, when the flakes began to drift across the garden at 7am, and I ran upstairs to wake him up to see. We pulled a coat and hat over his pyjamas, put on thick socks and wellies, and sent him out into the garden to play in the pathetically thin layer that formed across the lawn. By the time we'd eaten breakfast, and were ready to head out into the open for a second hit, the pavements were already slushy and the gutters were running with ice-melt. I wondered if that would be the peak of our snow experience until the next year.

But then it came: promised overnight on the weather forecast (for which we did not hold our breath), but there – definitely there – when we woke the next morning. This time, the garden was thick with it, covering all the weeds and bald grass, and making the whole place serene. School was certainly out, so we donned our winter gear and headed for the beach, where the snow sat in big marshmallows on top of the sea wall, and the edges of the grey sea had turned to slush. We built a snow seagull with a twig beak and a cockleshell bowtie, and rolled snowballs on the shingle. Later, we bought a new sledge (there were plenty in stock), and took it to Tankerton Slopes, which churned with laughing children pelting down the hill and staggering back up again with red cheeks. We watched four lads haring down in a kayak, which flew off the sea wall at the bottom, and crashed down onto the beach below.

A snow day is a wild day, a spontaneous holiday when all the tables are turned. This one had a bit of the spirit of Halloween, and a little of Christmas. It was wild and cosy at the same time; rebellious and heart-warming. Here was yet another liminal space, a crossing point between the mundane and the magical. Winter, it seems, is full of them: fleeting invitations to step out of the ordinary. Snow may be beautiful, but it is also a very adept con artist. It offers us a whole new world, but, just as we buy into it, it's whisked away.

★

When I see snow, I imagine Narnia. In many ways, C. S. Lewis offered us the Platonic ideal of snow: a thick, white, perfect layer over pine forests and quaint cottages. It is experienced by the children as a sudden transformation, after creeping through a wardrobe containing the warm fur coats they need to endure it. In *The Lion, the Witch and the Wardrobe*, snow is a nice surprise, at least for a while.

The book rings with the pleasures of snow: the yellow light of the lamp post reveals the purity of its whiteness, and we are presented with a world from which all ugliness has been removed, or at least con-cealed. Snow gives the children a chance to truly feel the cosy hospitality of Mr Tumnus and the Beavers, sheltered in the glow of the hearth and fed nursery food. The inhabitants of Narnia offer a warmth that is heightened by the contrasting cold outside.

There's no doubt that we are supposed to immediately perceive the White Witch's evil, but neither can we fail to perceive her glamour. Hers is an icy beauty, sharp and crystalline, speaking of the power to walk alongside the hardships of the cold. She seduces Edmund with Turkish delight and promises him magical powers. I've always thought that she carries a suggestion of Christmas: the sweets and food, the promise of gifts, but also the way that it forces children to dance with their own greed for a season, encouraged to desire worldly goods, but also scolded for wanting them too much, and with too much alacrity. She is the adult half of Christmas, perceived through a child's eyes, that slightly bitter edge which they can't help but notice as the grown-ups lecture them on the need to modify their demands, on the sacrifices they're making to stage their midwinter dreams. She is the mother dressing up for a party from which children are excluded, leaving the house masked in unfamiliar make-up and perfume; the adults lingering at the card table with drinks on Christmas evening, their cosy duties discharged. She is a glimpse of adult pleasures that they don't yet know how to crave.

But *The Lion, the Witch and the Wardrobe* is not alone in making the link between snow and the onset of adult knowingness. Susan's Cooper's *The Dark Is Rising* begins with a heavy fall of snow, enveloping Will Stanton's family cottage as he marks his eleventh birthday. Soon, he has time-slipped into a place where there is magic and prophecy and the looming threat of evil, and he is the only one who can save the world. Will comes of age in that snow. The same snowy segue takes us into John Masefield's *The Box of Delights*, where, during a Christmas break, the young hero Kay Harker witnesses a similar seepage in time. The snow brings not just a magical box that allows its holder to go swift or go small; it also brings about a muddling of an ancient pagan world and the bright certainties of Christianity. In the snow, time has lost its linearity, and deep history is present. Most of all, a young lad is forced to step into the role of an adult, with his parents absent and his guardian mysteriously vanished.

In children's literature, snowfall is the trigger for tables to turn. It creates a moment in which the usual adult protectors are easily incapacitated, and introduces a world in which children are agile and wild enough to survive. In the monumental battles these children face, the great are brought low and the weak rise up in power. This can only happen in the depths of midwinter, when the ordinary features of the world are erased. Snow vanquishes the mundane. It brings the everyday to a grinding halt, and delays our ability to address our dreary responsibilities. Snow opens up the reign of the children, high on their unexpected liberty, daredevil and impervious to the cold.

In this glistening white space, they get to feel the burgeoning of their own power.

★

On the second day of the snowfall, Bert didn't want to venture back out into the cold to play. He could no longer stand all the layers of clothing. He didn't want to wear a hat. He hated the way the wind stung his face. We watched *The Lego Movie*, and only at dusk did I persuade him to make the most of it and go outside again. We trudged down to the beach, now bathed in ethereal pink light. Pawprints dotted the snow, and the gulls seemed to confine themselves to the bare strip of shingle below the tideline. It must have been a lean week for them; they're used to picking up discarded scraps from the local chip shops and seafood cafes.

At the water's edge, we found that the shallows were thick and moving strangely. The salt water was nearly frozen, like rolling slush. Bert splashed through it in his wellies, but his feet were soon freezing, and we had to go home. There are years in recent memory when the sea at Whitstable has frozen over altogether: 1963, 1940 and 1929. The still waters of the harbour glaze even more frequently. Photographs from 1963 show the seabed a wasteland of cracked ice, looking for all the world like the documentation of a particularly intrepid polar expedition. At nearby Minster on the Isle of Sheppey, the sea froze in waves, as if some unseen hand simply arrested their motion, mid-undulation. The locals drew sledges across them, like some historical Frost Fair made real again. I nurture an ardent hope that the same thing will happen again one year, just for the chance to witness it, but I suspect it is not to be. Our cold snaps wane quickly.

When we awoke the next morning, a freeze had certainly happened, but not the one I dreamed of. Overnight, we must have had sleet, not warm enough to melt the snow, but wet and cold enough to form a sheen of thin ice over everything. We crackled through a thin layer of it on top of the snow, and the bare patches on the pavement looked as though they had been coated in glass. Every fence post, every street lamp and car, carried its sheen. Eden Phillpotts, the great chronicler of Dartmoor's natural lore, called this kind of weather an 'ammil', a corruption of 'enamel'. In 1918's *A Shadow Passes,* he described it as:

… a very rare, winter phenomenon produced by sudden freezing of heavy rain, or fog. It differs widely from a frost and displays the world of trees and stones and heather as though thinly coated with transparent glass. Should a morning sun flash on such a spectacle, the earth emerges as an unfamiliar and glittering dream.

When layered on top of snow, it feels less like a dream, and more like an entrenchment of hostilities. We were exhausted by the time we reached the seafront. The weather was no longer the benevolent provider of a winter wonderland. It had turned bitter. The sky above us was an angry grey, and the sea was a corresponding shade of ugly khaki, buffeted by a biting wind. Everything about the world around us seemed hard and unaccommodating, brutal and dangerous. The snow was doing nothing now, except making our lives more difficult.

'I want the snow to end,' said Bert.

'Yes,' I said. 'A couple of days was plenty.'

*

'I don't miss it,' says my friend Päivi Seppälä. 'It's a nuisance.'

We are drinking coffee in the kitchen of her baby, the LV21, a bright-red floating lightship that she and her husband Gary have converted into an arts centre. It's moored on the Thames at Gravesend, where recently a beluga whale has taken up residence. A migrant from the Arctic seas, it's tempting to believe that the whale has settled there to join Päivi, who also finds herself living further south than her native home.

Päivi is originally from Hamina, a small town in Finland that sits on the Baltic between Helsinki and St Petersburg. Hers is a landscape sandwiched between the sea and lakes, where, for six months of the year, winter descends.

'When the snow comes, it's actually a bit of a relief at first,' she says. 'With the short days, everything is so dark. And then snow falls, and it's like someone's turned on the lights.'

Her family get out separate winter curtains, not with the aim of keeping warm, but instead to try to let in the light that reflects from the snow cover. The cold months are not a period of hunkering down in the house; it's too easy to do nothing in the winter, and to endure the terrible toll that takes on your mental health. Instead, winter is a time to fight the isolation that snow brings.

Life in the deep freeze, as Päivi describes it, is not full of wintery romance, but is actually a mass of inconveniences and frustrations. With snow on the ground for three months of each year, schools never close for cold weather (although the children are allowed to play indoors if temperature falls below −25°C), and taking days off work isn't an option. Everything must continue to run. This means spending ages digging out and warming up the car each morning, and wrapping up in warm layers for the shortest journeys. Simple tasks take a long time and carry risks. Roads are ploughed across the frozen waterways, but they're not always safe, and people – including Päivi's father and sister at different points in time – sometimes fall through the ice. Everybody carries warm clothes and boots in their car, just in case. The risk of getting stranded is real. Mobile phones use up all their energy in keeping warm, and run out of charge so quickly that they're nearly useless.

You take vitamin D and try to get outside as much as you can. Some people cycle with special snow tyres; others ski. Keeping the house warm means that your electricity bill can rocket to the equivalent of £2,000 a month in the winter. It's a necessary evil, but it makes the air so dry indoors that your skin turns to scales. You drink gallons of coffee in an effort to stay awake, and try not to succumb to the drinking culture that damages the health of so many Finns. When you go for a night out, you have to agree to a policy of 'no man left behind'. Passing out in the snow is not an option. You grow up hearing tales of people who died due to one poor decision made after a night out in the cold.

My tendency to think of snow as a bit of light relief is a privilege. To those who live with it, snow is plain hard work. The British incompetence in the face of a brief cold snap is a national joke, but it's also the by-product of our not actually having to make the effort to cope. We treat snow like a dirty weekend, and then head back to work again, grumbling about the slush.

'So is there nothing you like about snow?' I say, slightly deflated.

'Oh yes,' says Päivi. 'When it's really cold, the snow makes a lovely noise underfoot, and it's like the air is full of stars. I miss being able to freeze my washing on the line.'

'Does it actually dry?' I ask.

'Not really,' she says, 'but it smells incredible afterwards. You can hang out your woollens to kill the bacteria, rather than washing them. It's good for them.'

'And you sauna?'

'Yes, we do. And we sometimes roll naked in the snow afterwards. You get a garden full of rude-looking snow angels. Sometimes we cut a hole in the ice so we can dip into the water. You put down rag rugs so your feet don't freeze. I have to scream to get in but it's …

refreshing. We have candles and ice cream and coffee. We all have our coping mechanisms.'

'But you wouldn't go back?'

'No. This,' she gestures to her boat, which has taken years of hard work to restore, involving huge social and financial sacrifices, 'is much easier.'

At that moment, her teenage niece, who is visiting from Hamina, wanders in. 'Tell Katherine what you think about the winter,' says Päivi.

'I hate it,' says Luna. 'I hate the cold.'

'How many times has your car got stuck now?' says Päivi.

'Twice,' says Luna. 'Once I had to be dragged off the ice by a tractor. The other time I spent an hour digging my car out of the snow.'

'And she's only just passed her test,' says Päivi, with a slight roll of her eyes.

COLD WATER

FOR THE LAST THREE YEARS, I have taken part in the annual Whitstable New Year sea swim. It goes something like this: a crowd of us mill around on the beach for as long as we can possibly get away with it, then we run in, scream and run back out again. It's all over very quickly.

I don't really take part for the experience; I take part to be able to say I've done it. I undertake the most complex labyrinth of planning first, and on the first year turned up in both a rash vest and a wetsuit, with a swimming costume underneath, sea shoes and a woolly hat. I've since ditched the rash vest. For the aftermath, I bring three large towels and a dressing gown, a tracksuit, a flask of hot tea and a pre-mixed Bloody Mary. I'm in the water for no more than fifteen seconds. The best part is getting dressed again, while toasting my own bravery.

But then, part of my dream of living on the coast was that I'd swim all year round. I read Iris Murdoch's *The Sea, The Sea* in my early twenties, and had always thought that I could be the kind of doughty soul who got into the water every day and blazed a few determined strokes through the waves. If not, what was even the point of being there? I let myself off for the first year, because we had only arrived in town in November, and it seemed like a bad idea to start when the water was already extremely cold. Best to begin in the summer, and gradually acclimatise, I thought. Then I'll barely notice.

I swam in the summer a bit, but not enough. I couldn't really seem to get the hang of the tides. After the first few months, we moved from our rented house on the beach to something more affordable, five minutes' walk away. It meant that, on several occasions, I put on my swimming costume and headed to the beach, only to find the sea so far out that I'd have to wade through acres of mud to reach it. Once or twice, I even performed this feat, only to find the water ankle-deep. I realised I needed a tide table, but instead of buying the sensible one that they sell in pretty much every local pub and cafe, I managed to buy an elaborate one from an art gallery, which revealed to me the tides of the whole south-east coast if I aligned a wheel and cross-checked it against a complicated table. It was all the most un-believable nuisance. I gave up.

This year, my friend Emma asked if I'd accompany her on her own New Year swim, as part of a bucket list of challenges she was trying to complete around her fortieth birthday. I was supposed to be able to offer the benefit of my cold water experience, and I didn't like to confess that it amounted to nothing. There was some-thing very different about the whole enterprise now that it was just the two of us. I lent her my spare wetsuit and assured her that she would survive. At the same time, I felt a bodily reluctance to enter the sea. I had the sense that swimming (if you could call it that) with the other thrashing bodies at New Year probably has a warming effect, which we would lack on our own. In addition, this swim would require my own willpower to get in. Last year, I only had to follow the herd.

We ended up driving the short distance to the sea-front, reasoning that we could quickly get back into the car and put the heater on full blast when we were done. I won't lie: I memorised the symptoms of hypo-thermia, just in case. We crunched onto the beach and made our reckoning with the water. It was 6°C, and drizzling. The water was closer to 3°C. The sky was a uniform white and the sea a churning grey. 'Right,' I said, 'come on. The quicker we do this, the quicker we get back home.'

Emma counted down – three, two, one – and we ran, stumbling over the shingle and into the waves, emitting a battle cry that turned into a squeal as we hit the water. I got in thigh-deep before deciding to launch myself forwards to take a few strokes. That was when the cold hit me: a vast, bitter wall that kicked the breath out of my lungs. It was so absolute, so vicious. I flickered my arms in a feeble attempt at breast stroke, but it was impossible. The freezing water drew me tight together, like a brittle rubber band. It felt something like fear. I had no scope for movement, or even to suck in air. It was as though the sea had gripped me in an icy fist, and was crushing me. I found my feet and ran back out of the water again, with Emma in hot pursuit.

Afterwards, standing on the beach with towels piled around me and a cup of tea in my hand, something strange happened. Gazing back at the water, I had the urge to do it all over again, to go back and exist in those few, crystalline seconds in the intense cold. My blood seemed to sparkle in my veins. I was certain that I could conquer it a second time around, could tolerate a little longer in that frozen claw.

'That was brilliant,' I gasped.

★

'The effect starts as soon as I approach the beach. My body knows what's coming, and I start to warm up.

Just thinking about getting into the sea makes my temperature rise from thirty-seven degrees to thirty-eight.'

As I speak to Dorte Lyager over Skype, she's sitting in her car, her face glowing with what I suspect is the aftermath of a swim. She's an experienced cold-water swimmer, getting into the sea all year round in her native Jutland in the northernmost tip of Denmark. And she does it to survive.

'Seven to eight degrees is the ideal temperature,' she says. 'I can put my head under and feel truly surrounded with cold water. When I come up again, everything is washed away.'

Dorte is a member of a Polar Bear Club, a group of people committed to sea swimming all year round; around twenty of them gather at seven o'clock each morning to swim. These clubs are dotted all around the coast in Denmark, often offering changing facilities and a sauna to warm up in afterwards. She's been a member for around three years now, and although the circumstances that brought her there were desperate, she's now an extraordinary example of the power of spending time in the cold.

'In October 2013, I was at the end of the road,' she tells me. 'For the last ten years, I had been really sick with recurring hypermania and depression. I'd tried every single drug. My psychiatrist kept telling me that it was a matter of finding the right combination; the aim was to become *rask*. It's a complicated word. It means well – healthy – but also fixed. I'd been waiting a decade for the medication to mend me. The change came when I stopped believing it could.'

That pivotal point came, for Dorte, when she found a fresh perspective on her situation that changed the way she conceptualised it. Feeling that, yet again, the drugs weren't working, she made an appointment with her GP, and happened to see a doctor she'd never met before. He told her that they could keep tinkering with her medication, but it would never solve everything. 'This isn't about you getting fixed,' he said, 'this is about you living the best life you can with the parameters that you have.'

He was the first person to ever say that, and the effect was profound. Perhaps a year before – perhaps even less than that – she wouldn't have been ready to hear it, but that day she was. It should have been devastating to face the idea that she would always be bipolar; after all, it was currently having a terrible impact on her health and happiness. But for Dorte, this was not a moment of lost hope, but an invitation to finally adapt to what she needed. 'Nobody had ever said to me: you need to live a life that you can cope with, not the one that other people want. Start saying "no". Just do one thing a day. No more than two social events in a week. I owe my life to him.'

Dorte had always been the kind of person who fixed everything for everyone else. She wasn't just trying to get by; she was trying to carry out super-human feats of generosity, sorting things out for all the local mothers, filling her family life with events and activities, and constantly having her house stuffed with people. Suddenly, she was being invited to look after herself in order to survive.

First of all, she found a public spa and started going there twice a month to relax. It was expensive, but she knew that she needed to learn how to take care of herself. She would sit in the sauna, and then dip into the cold plunge pool, repeating the cycle over and over again. But after her first few visits, she realised that it was the cold that she was craving, rather than the comforting heat. Something was happening to her brain; something that made it feel clear and calm for the first time in years.

'When I'm stressed, it is like my brain has turned to porridge and it's coming out of my ears. The drugs for my bipolar never really stopped that. Cold water does.' A biologist by training, Dorte began to look at the recent research into her condition, and came across the work of Edward Bullmore, a Cambridge neuroscientist who believes that depression is caused by inflammation in the brain. In this context, the effect of the cold made sense. 'I'm treating my brain like an inflamed joint,' she says.

This has led to some fairly elaborate attempts to get her cold fixes in the summer. Dorte bought herself an old agricultural tank, and she now drives to the local harbour to fill her trailer with 200kg of ice each summer, which she tops up with 400 litres of water to create an ice bath whose temperature hovers at around 3°C to 4°C. It sounds like an extraordinary amount of effort to go to for something that most of us would find deeply unpleasant, but Dorte has learned to love it. At first, she could only manage to stay in for three minutes at a time, but she gradually built up to half an hour. 'I just love the feeling it gives me,' she says. 'I feel so calm and relaxed. My inner voice doesn't say *Get out!* like everyone else's does. It says: *Finally. At last.*

'While I'm in the water, I'm just laughing and laughing. All my automatic thoughts switch off, and I'm just in the water. I always dip my head under, just to make sure the cold gets to my brain. And afterwards, I can't remember what was even worrying me. A switch has been flicked. It's a physical thing.'

But Dorte doesn't simply mean that she's found a therapeutic practice that keeps her symptoms at bay. 'I feel like I've been cured,' she says. 'A bipolar episode is defined as a manic high lasting at least seven days, and a depressive phase lasting for at least two weeks. I might now get depressed for a day, and go to the beach, and then I've dealt with it.'

She doesn't seek to minimise or diminish the risk that she faces, or the potential it has to harm her all over again. But she's found a way of keeping it under control that's so effective – and so pleasurable in the meantime – that it makes everything feel easy for the first time in her life. 'I now think of it as mental influenza,' she says. 'I don't power on through, I don't put up a facade, and I don't keep it in. I take a couple of days off, and look after myself until I'm well again. I go to the sea, make sure I'm getting some good nutrition, cancel all my appointments, and rest until I'm better. I know what to do.'

This regime means that she has now achieved something that she could never have imagined a decade ago. 'Last year, I got depressed again. I found myself crying on the way to the beach, and only feeling better on the way home. I went to my psychiatrist, and he suggested to me that I was over-medicated and that it was time to cut down my drugs. This made me incredibly anxious, because I'd never managed without the meds before. But we planned a supported retreat, and the lower my dose, the better I felt.' She is now medication-free.

'It's not a quick fix,' she says. 'I'm still not the same as someone without a diagnosis in the first place. This has been a long journey for me, and swimming is just one of the changes I've made. I've cut out sugar, I make sure I get plenty of alone time, I go on long walks, and I've stopped saying yes to everybody. I've cut down my working hours. All of these things make a buffer, and I say I like to keep my buffer broad. Sometimes problems come up that narrow my buffer, and then I have to make sure I build it up again. Keeping well is almost a full-time job. But I have a wonderful life.'

★

Not long after New Year, I am copied in to a Facebook group full of names I don't know, with the message, 'I think this is one for Katherine.'

As I scroll through the speech bubbles, I see that somebody is trying to set up a group of people who are willing to swim through the year, whatever the weather. Most of the invitees are saying something along the lines of: 'You're completely crazy and I might perhaps be willing to join you in the summer.'

I say, 'Oh, yes please!'

I meet Margo Selby on the beach on the day after the first snow. We had a small flurry of snow the previous morning, and standing on the shore with a swimming costume under my clothes, I can see delicate drifts still clustering around the edges of the wave-breaks in the shady spots that the winter sun never reaches.

'I'm so glad you came,' says Margo. 'I've been trying to go in on my own, but it's so hard to work up the nerve each time.'

I look at the sea, and the frozen beach beneath my feet, and suggest that this is an understatement. There is ice on the seaweed, and the wood-grain of the groynes is picked out in frost. My breath floats in front of me in an ominous white cloud. If there wasn't someone there to witness my cowardice, I would already be in the nearest cafe, ordering a hot chocolate. But here I am, clutching my wetsuit, and wondering about leaving my bobble hat on as I swim.

'I won't stay in for long,' I say.

'Neither will I,' says Margo. 'I'm trying to build up to three minutes.'

I take off my coat and my clothes, and feel the air bite at my bare flesh. This is complete insanity – not just the act of the swim, but the compulsion I feel to do it; the conviction that it will somehow do me good, that it is necessary and wise. I pull on my wetsuit and shoes, and notice that Margo is wearing nothing but a swimming costume and some black socks.

'They're neoprene,' she says. 'Five millimetres thick.' She has gloves, too, the kind that divers wear. 'I asked some women who are swimming the Channel. They said that you have to protect your extremities from, you know … frostbite.'

It is better not to think about frostbite at this point. I reiterate that I will really not be spending very long in the water, and we both turn to confront the sludge-green sea. Getting into the water seems a complete impossibility. But then we are both striding towards it purposefully, and my shins are wet, and then my thighs. I fall forwards to submerge my body, and realise that we are both sounding off without even thinking about it, not screaming exactly, but singing through the sting of the cold, and the sensation that the breath has been knocked out of us. This is no place for inhibition, or toughing it out. We both call through the thrill of our discomfort.

'Breathe!' says Margo, and I haul air into my lungs, and decide that I can survive three breast-stokes before I get out again, so that's what I do: one, two … and it's really only two and a half before I'm on my feet and running out again to huddle under my towel. I was in for perhaps forty-five seconds, although it feels as though time was warped by the experience, so it could easily have been shorter. I watch Margo swimming with her head upright, a look of intent on her face and her cheeks puffing with the effort. I feel safe now, having been in and got out again; I have survived. It is obvious, in retrospect, that staying in a little longer would only have been a matter of nerve.

Soon, Margo is out too, and standing next to me, drying off. My skin tingles with the memory of cold. 'I think I have the measure of it now,' I say. 'I came out because I didn't think it was possible to stay in. But as soon as I was out, I could see that it was fine. I want to go back in.'

'Tomorrow?' says Margo.

'Tomorrow,' I say.

The second day, I set the timer on my phone, and find that I can stay in for nearly five minutes if I put aside the fear that I will suddenly die of hypothermia. I've done my research, and know that it's a slower process than that, which is oddly reassuring. I know that I am to get straight out if I start shivering in the water, but also if I start feeling warm again. For as long as I'm feeling the cold, I'm relatively safe. On that second day, I learn that my thumb joints will send me a clear signal when it's time to give in: in this most fleshless part of my body, my bones feel the cold as sharp pain, which soon abates when I am out of the water.

In Whitstable, you can only swim in the two hours surrounding the high tide, and each high tide is twelve and a half hours apart, which means that the time you can swim shifts by an hour each day. Our 11am swim on that first Sunday became a midday swim on Monday, and then moved through one, two and three o'clock in the afternoon, until the short February days would nearly have us swimming in the dark. I was determined to last out the week, swimming every day to force myself to acclimatise, so I went back to the beach again and again, and fought my own instinct to stay warm and dry.

Over the course of that week, the sea temperature hovered between 5 and 6°C, and I grew accustomed to the strange bodily transformations that happen in icy water. Getting out, your skin turns bright red, not the colour of a blush or a hot flush, but the specific, deep orange of Heinz tomato soup. I learn to love that colour, my signal of having endured something so unlike anything else in my days. Once I'm warm and dry, I always begin to shiver in a way that isn't entirely unpleasant. It is clear that my body is warming itself up again, something that I haven't required it to do for years. It makes me feel alive, and I'm not afraid of it, because Margo experiences it too. I have deliberately thrown my body into a kind of crisis to force it to find an equilibrium again. It feels good to test my physical limits in such an invigorating way. Best of all, the blood tingles in my veins for hours afterwards, as though I have been infused with some magnificent serum.

On the fourth day, I jettison the wetsuit and plunge in wearing just my swimsuit, and I am surprised to find that I feel fine. By now, I've learned to breathe through the initial thirty seconds when my chest feels tight, and to simply acknowledge the cold. On the fifth day, I stay in for ten minutes straight, astonished at how quickly I have adapted. We bob side by side in the grey water, and fall in to the pattern that we have already established of joyous, stream-of-consciousness chatter. To an outsider, we must look as high as a pair of kites, trilling at the wonder of the cold.

'This is wonderful!' we say. 'This is amazing!' We are completely enchanted by our own bravery, by the way that we've stepped out of the everyday world and into this alternative space. Our town, with all its stresses and responsibilities, rises at the other side of the beach, but we have put a barrier in place to stop it reaching us, just for now. Nobody could get us here; nobody would dare. Dog walkers stop on the shore to watch us, pointing and shaking their heads. We have crossed a glorious, brave, unspoken line. We decide that we like to swim at Seasalter best of all, because there, on the deserted beach, away from houses and shielded by a high sea wall, we can just strip off our swimming costumes when we get out, and stand naked on the shingle for a while as we dry off. I don't have the sort of body that makes me comfortable in a bikini on a summer's day, but in the winter, I can show my skin to the sea and feel like I'm part of its elemental power.

Immersion in cold water has been shown to increase levels of dopamine (the neurotransmitter that stimulates the brain's reward and pleasure centres) by 250 per cent, and a 2000 study by Šrámek et al. published in the *European Journal of Applied Physiology* found that regular winter swimming significantly decreased tension and fatigue, as well as negative states associated with memory and mood, and improved swimmers' sense of general well-being. It's no surprise, then, that we felt good, but the effects felt more than physiological. Getting into the sea on days when the temperature hovered around zero was an act of defiance against our own woes. By doing a resilient thing, we felt more resilient. That circular process of being resilient and feeling resilient kept us afloat.

I, who generally prefer to do everything alone if I can possibly help it, came to see how this was only made possible by a contract between us. The fear of stepping into the water – of even getting to the beach in the first place – never subsided, but having a partner in crime made it harder to avoid. We challenged each other to find half an hour in our schedules in which to swim, and reminded each other, as we stood in our swimming costumes accumulating goosepimples, that we actually enjoyed ourselves once we were in. It always seemed hard to believe, but it was an act of faith that we undertook together. 'Of all the things I do in my day,' said Margo one afternoon, 'this is the only time that I don't think I ought to be anywhere else.'

Encountering the extremes of cold drew us both into that most clichéd space, The Moment, forcibly pulling our minds away from ruminating on the past or future, or tilling over an endless to-do list. We had to tend to our bodies right here, right now, ever watchful that the cold would not encroach too far. More than that, the sea offered us an endless number of gifts to observe. It was different every day, sometimes ridged with waves, sometimes millpond-flat. It turned pewter under pale skies, and craggy grey under storm clouds. Still days left it clear and blue as the Mediterranean. Sometimes black-headed gulls or herring gulls bobbed alongside us; sometimes a cormorant would swoop past; sometimes a flock of sanderlings would flit by, low over the water, chirping as they went. The occasional dog swam out to meet us, and one day I watched, helpless, as one ran off with my towel. There were days when the water felt silky, and days when it was thick at the edges, nearly slush. We began to feel how the sea would fall slack at the height of the tide, as if pausing to take a breath before it began to flood away again. It tasted saltier just before the high tide, and fresher after it turned. We speculated that the river was diluting it.

Soon, others joined us, drawn in by our crazed enthusiasm, and we became coaches, urging people to grapple with their fears, teaching them to breathe through those first seconds, to get out when their thumbs ached. The sea was like a shortcut to intimacy, and while we were all riding our cold-water highs, we found ourselves blurting out all the troubles of our current lives. We swam alongside each other's anxieties about money, our parents, our children; we dispensed with social niceties and started talking as soon as we hit the water. We let the cold unburden us of our own personal winters, just for a few moments, and freely shared our darkest, most vulnerable thoughts. We talked, barely knowing each other's names, and then wriggled back into our everyday clothes and walked away to our everyday lives, shivering a little, feeling that sparkle in our veins. The brevity of our swims was an ideal window in which to loosen our tongues, and then to tighten them again. We buttoned ourselves back up and went home.

At the end of that first month, we lit a bonfire on the beach just as the sun was setting, and dried off in its warmth as our children played. We drank wine and toasted marshmallows, and we attracted some new recruits, complete strangers who walked up to say, 'Have you been in? Was it cold? How did you manage? Can I join you one day?'

We smiled and said, *Welcome.*

MARCH

SURVIVAL

A S A CHILD, I HAD a copy of Aesop's fable of the Ant and the Grasshopper in shiny yellow hardback. It told the story of a rather easy-going grasshopper, who spends the summer watching ants labouring away to store food for winter. Meanwhile, he lazes in the sun and strums his guitar. He was, in my edition, an artefact of his time: the very picture of the work-shy hippie, presumably conjured up in the decade before I was born to illustrate a lesson about the perils of the urge to turn on, tune in, drop out.

In my memory (and it will remain a memory, be-cause I can no longer find it), he has a little banter with the ant while he watches the intense effort going on around him: *Hey dude, why so busy? Why not just enjoy the beautiful summer?* The ant's answer only becomes truly clear when winter comes, and the grasshopper is starving, and huddling against the encroaching winds:

the wise do not have time for the trivialities of leisure. They are engaged in the business of survival.

I now know that this version had been expanded a great deal from the Aesopian original, which is compact to the point of brutality. Here, we don't encounter the grasshopper's summer at all; we are landed straight in his winter, where the ants are busy drying grain that they had stored since the summertime. The grasshopper merely passes by, and, starving hungry, begs for food. In George Fyler Townsend's translation, published in the mid-nineteenth century and considered to be the standard edition, the ants (who speak as a collective) are blunt in their reply.

'Why did you not treasure up food during the summer?' they ask.

'I had not leisure enough,' says the grasshopper. 'I passed the days in singing.'

'If you were foolish enough to sing all the summer,' scoff the ants, 'you must dance supperless to bed in the winter.'

Even as a child, I remember being outraged by the ants' behaviour. It seemed like the moral of the story was all wrong. I still feel the shock of it now, the brutality of those ants, and the simple need of the grasshopper. This went against everything I'd learned at school about Christian charity. He has, after all, only done what a grasshopper is supposed to do

– sing – and the ants, in turn, have fulfilled their own biological imperative. At worst, he has made a simple mistake, which is unlikely to be repeated again; but it always struck me that the ants had missed an opportunity to make a productive trade: the entertainment of a singing grasshopper while they worked, in return for a small amount of food in the winter.

As an adult, the story takes on an even darker tint. The grasshopper, after all, is not a creature that over-winters; rather, it tends to survive only genetically, in the form of its eggs. The ants, therefore, are not being asked to sustain an extra body across the whole of winter; they are instead denying the final request of a dying creature. Did Aesop know this? Does the story, in part, attempt to account for the disappearance of grasshoppers over the winter? Are we therefore being presented with a kind of tableau that represents a much larger whole, the denial of one grasshopper's needs forming a pattern that's reproduced across whole eco-systems? Whichever way you look at it, the ants are mean and sanctimonious, possibly also genocidal.

But taking my tongue back out of my cheek, it's impossible not to taste the resonances of the ants' stance. It would not have been lost on the Victorians, and certainly chimes with many voices in contemporary politics, too. The grasshopper is the universal vagrant: the layabout, the benefit-scrounger, the profligate who splurges what little money they have on things they don't need. The people who think the rules don't apply to them; the cheats and the criminals; the mothers who, we're told, have babies just to procure a council flat, or who sit at home on state maternity pay, just to avoid paying their fair part. The slackers and the hangers-on, the adult children who refuse to flee their cosy nest, and the millennials who are so busy buying avocado toast that they have to rely on the Bank of Mum and Dad. The economic migrants, the refugees, the gypsies and travellers who live lightly. This great, amorphous crowd, knocking on the doors of the decent folk who work for a living, and who always pay their way.

The grasshopper is symbolic of such an array of folk devils that it's difficult to know where to start; his identity shifts, I suspect, with each generation, each social class, each town or city feeling its own threats. The ants, meanwhile, are static. They are the simple, upstanding citizens who behave themselves. They save for rainy days, instead of relying on the handouts of others. They keep themselves to themselves, and look after their own. They are a projection of how we so often think we ought to live, but also a model for a life we've collectively failed to achieve, over and over again, across the entire history of humanity. The ants are not real, or not on a mass scale;

they are an *if only*. If only everyone could be the ants. If only we were all so forward-thinking and responsible. If only the grasshoppers of this world could be so simply dispatched.

I will give you an alternative *if only*. If only life were so stable, happy and predictable as to produce ants instead of grasshoppers, year in, year out. The truth is that we all have ant years and grasshopper years; years when we are able to prepare and save, and years where we need a little extra help. Our true flaw lies not in failing to store up enough resources to cope with the grasshopper years, but in believing that each grasshopper year is an anomaly, visited only on us, due to our unique human failings.

★

Back in September, I went for a walk behind the studio where I go to write. I have what's essentially a cupboard in an old farm building that's otherwise populated with visual artists. I can't really justify any more space; a cupboard is all I need, and a narrow shelf on which to perch my laptop. In any case, I tend to spend more time walking than actually writing, striking off through the farm and into the fields beyond, where I can join onto the North Downs Way and walk to Canterbury in an hour if I want to. Heading in the opposite direction are a string of little country pubs, where I can sit for a while and pretend I'm gathering my wits about me.

But mostly, I tend to catch the air for a few moments before I return to my screen again. In one direction, there is a walnut orchard; in another, a field of blackcurrant bushes; but mostly, there are rows and rows of apple trees, and that is where I went on this day, past the stacked wooden crates that looked ready to take the fruit to market, and through a patch of long grass, already dotted with the skeletons of various umbellifers, now wasted into fragile starbursts. The sun doesn't reach this spot until the afternoon, and there was a heavy dew still in place, lighting up the spider webs and glossing the apples.

I was heading for a row of beehives, so often the object of my walk. All summer, I'd enjoyed listening to their hum, and watching the industrious commotion around them. But today, I noticed something slightly different. Bisecting the hive was a sheet of newspaper, dividing the top half from the bottom. The bees were floating around it as if on invisible wires, pinging in the stiff lines of their flight. Others clustered on the surface, crawling over the surface of the paper, exploring the seam it made with their hive. They were clearly curious. And I was curious, too. What could a sheet of newspaper do for a colony of bees?

When I asked on Twitter, it appeared that everyone knew the answer except me: the keeper is combining two hives, salvaging the stronger bees from a weak colony whose queen is beginning to fail, and which may not otherwise survive the winter. The newspaper allows these bees to join another queen without causing the kind of fighting that could damage both colonies. It works like this: the beekeeper will stack a weakening colony on top of a strong one, with the paper in between. The bees will smell each other, and set about chewing through, but by the time they finish the task, the weaker bees will have picked up the scent of their new queen and lost interest in fighting. By the time the beekeeper opens the hive again, there will be nothing left of the newspaper except for a ring of it where the two hive boxes meet, and the two groups of bees will be living together in harmony.

But what caught my attention was a comment from Al Warren, a man so enthusiastic about beekeeping that he's managed to persuade his local primary school to host three of his hives. 'I don't usually bother with the newspaper method,' he says. 'Honeybees have got a pretty foolproof methods of surviving the winter for themselves. They're wintering machines.'

'When you think about bees,' he tells me later, 'don't treat them as individuals. A colony of bees is a single superorganism. They act as one.' And, although it's easy to think of bees as summer beings, adapted to drifting around flowers on hot days, their whole year is oriented in the opposite direction. Most of a bee's activity is directed towards its colony surviving the winter. They spend half the year preparing for it, and half the year living it. Every April, they emerge from their hive, and start all over again.

A honeybee colony consists of something in the region of 30,000 to 40,000 bees – one queen, a few hundred male drones, and tens of thousands of female worker bees, plus many more eggs and larvae. The sole role of the drones is to mate with the queen early in her life, after which time she stores millions of sperm in her body and uses this to lay around 2,000 fertilised eggs per day. The workers carry out all the other tasks, working through a defined roster of roles at different stages in their lives. When they are young, they keep the hive clean, and then they graduate to a succession of other duties, depending on their experience and expendability: they tend to larvae and young bees; they look after the queen; they put nectar into the cells, make wax to produce new honeycomb, make the honey itself, and serve as guard bees. The final role of their lives is to go out foraging, because this is the most dangerous task of all, and older bees are expend-able. We probably only ever see ancient bees, sent out on risky missions to gather nectar for carbs and pollen for protein. Al says that you can tell the age of a bee by the intensity of its sting – the older bees have far more potent venom. It seems only fair, given the risks they have to take.

The way that bees achieve this carefully balanced social order is by behaving like cells in a larger body. 'You or I,' says Al, 'have bodies that regulate themselves. We don't even have to think about all the things that keep us alive; they just happen. That's exactly what a hive does. It keeps itself alive.' This regulation is achieved by using pheromones, vibration and touch to communicate the needs of the colony so that individual bees can act on its requirements. Everything is automatic; the engine maintains itself. And it's nearly fail-safe.

To store a source of carbohydrates for winter, the bees make honey. If they simply stored the nectar, it would ferment, so they produce an enzyme that turns it into honey by splitting the molecules to extract most of the water. Should a bee arrive at the honeycomb to find all the cells full, its bulging stomach will trigger the production of wax so that it can immediately make a new cell. Nothing in the hive is left to chance. If, for example, a nurse bee dies, then the larvae it was tending will emit a pheromone that makes each adult bee regress a stage, so that the role of nurse is fulfilled once more. We sometimes think of bees as models of good management, but they're more efficient than that. 'If you cut your finger,' says Al, 'your body will automatically deploy the right cells to heal it. It's just the same with bees.'

All of this gargantuan effort – the collective work of an unfathomable number of bees – is pointed towards the winter. Being a honeybee is a mass enterprise, and even in the bee world they are unique in trying to wait out the cold season in such large numbers. Bumblebees, for example, form nests of around five hundred in the summer, but in the winter they drastically reduce their numbers. The new queens (bumblebee colonies can have more than one) will mate and then hibernate in a safe place, such as a hole in the ground. The rest of the colony will die, including the older queens. In the spring, a new nest is built from scratch, populated with the eggs laid by the queens.

But honeybees attempt to live out the winter preserving the maximum number of lives, so that they can leap straight into mass honey production from the moment the first flowers appear. In autumn, the male drones are sacrificed because they're no longer of any use, and would otherwise just be hungry mouths to feed; the queen has stopped laying eggs. The worker bees eject them from the hive, and those who refuse to go are stung to death. Many worker bees also die of exhaustion at the end of the summer. But even in these reduced numbers, the hive needs to sustain countless lives. Therefore, they have evolved an ingenious way to keep warm.

The honeybee can disconnect its wings from its flight muscles – rather like putting the car into neutral – and then rev those muscles to become heater bees. In the depths of the hive in winter, the bees cluster together to retain heat, and these cold-blooded creatures take turns to act as little radiators, sometimes reaching 45°C, which is seven degrees higher than human body. Even on the coldest days, a beehive will retain a temperature of 35°C in the very centre. When each heater bee gets exhausted, another bee takes over. The superorganism is maintained until spring. Honey fuels the whole process.

★

Even as I write about bees, I'm urging myself to be cautious. It's beguilingly easy to see them as tiny analogies for human beings, the crisp bustle of the bee colony serving as an example to us all. In a mere slip of the pen, I could fall into the tired old trope: the bees are models of industry. Be more like the bees.

Indeed, the sociobiologist E. O. Wilson suggests that we're more similar to bees than most people would dare to imagine. He offers bees and ants as prime examples of 'eusocial' creatures: those that organise their labour cooperatively for the greater good of their society, and he suggests that humans show similar behaviour, just organised differently. Humans may go about their daily business without the help of the pheromone trails or physical specialisations that we find in social insects, but Wilson believes that our tendency towards cooperation is just as hardwired.

The idea of the human machine – a natural order of things that could function as smoothly as a beehive if only we could cut away the bad habits we've got into over the course of our existence on this earth – has long attracted many thinkers on both the Left and the Right. Whether your taste runs to military efficiency, with no space left for the whining neediness of individuals, or flat, egalitarian structures in which everyone gets what they need rather than what they want, then there's a beehive metaphor for you. In *Bee Wise* (1913), for example, the socialist author Charlotte Perkins Gilman imagined an idealised society founded by women, where domestic labour was shared on a mass scale and the careful industry of women produced superior leather, cotton and fruit. But to marry, they had to 'prove clean health – for a high grade of motherhood was the continuing ideal of the group.'

At the other end of the political spectrum, Mussolini was fond of evoking the beehive to describe the ideal functioning of Fascism. 'It is usual to speak of the Fascist objective as the "beehive state", which does grave injustice to bees,' wrote George Orwell in *The Road to Wigan Pier*. 'A world of rabbits ruled by stoats would be nearer the mark.'

But before we're too enchanted by the machine-like efficiency of the utopian human beehive, we must remember the true lives of bees. They are certainly astonishing. Their specialisation – and their sheer will to survive – is miraculous. But their lives are also full of stark efficiencies. In the middle of winter, the area around my favourite beehive is littered with the corpses of the bees that were no longer useful – the most expendable, who were sent on the dangerous mission of foraging; the male drones who were ejected from the hive at the end of their useful lives.

Let us not aspire to be like ants and bees. We can draw enough wonder from their intricate systems of survival without modelling ourselves on them whole-sale. Humans are not eusocial; we are not nameless units in a superorganism, mere cells that are expend-able when we have reached the end of our useful lives. The life of a sociable insect has nothing to say about us. Our lives take different shapes: we do not work in a linear progression through fixed roles like the hon-eybee. We are not consistently useful to the world at large. We talk about the complexity of the hive, but human societies are infinitely more complex, full of choices and mistakes, periods of glory and seasons of utter despair. Some of us make highly visible, elaborate contributions to the whole; some of us are part of the ticking mechanics of the world, the incremental wealth of small gestures. All of it matters. All of it weaves the wider fabric that binds us.

In the eusocial hive, we would only have to undergo our first wintering in order to be driven out – for the greater good. And it may well be true that a bee can't recover, but a human can. We may sometimes drift through years in which we feel like a negative presence in the world, but we come back again, not only restored, but bringing more than we brought before: more wisdom, more compassion, a greater capacity to reach deep into our roots and know that we will find water.

Usefulness, in itself, is a useless concept when it comes to humans. I don't think we were ever meant to think about others in terms of their use to us. We keep pets just for the pleasure of looking after them; we voluntarily feed these extra mouths and scoop up excrement in little plastic bags, and declare it relaxing. We channel our adoration towards the most helpless citizens of all – babies and children – for reasons that have nothing to do with their future utility. We flourish on caring, on doling out love. The most helpless members of our families and communities are what stick us together. It's how we thrive. Our winters are social glue.

★

The ants aren't entirely wrong, though: winter does carry its own labours, and preparations can be made for future periods of dearth that we can't quite yet imagine. We have always been instructed to save, of course, although many of us find it impossible to stretch budgets that far these days. Even if we do save, it's of limited use. My own savings were obliterated in one fairly brutal sweep when a sickly pregnancy left me unable to work, and then childcare cost more than I earned. It doesn't take much: ordinary things, nothing more. The margins of adult life are narrow.

We are told to live within our means, but there are times when, frankly, I feel that 'my means' would be a caravan on waste ground. Instead, I suspect that most of us have periods of feast and famine in our lives, and, increasingly, we spend the feast years paying off the debts of the famine. *It's only money*, as a friend of mine often says with a sigh.

But the works of winter are more intricate than the simple storing up of supplies, which are then run down until the summer replenishes them. Cooped up in our hives, with cold winds blasting at the roof, we are invited into the industry of the dark season, when there is nothing else to do but keep our hands moving. Winter is a time for the quiet arts of making: for knitting and sewing, baking and simmering, repairing and restoring our homes.

In the high summer, we want to be outside and active; in winter, we are called inside, and here we attend to all the detritus of the summer months, when we were too busy to take the necessary care. Winter is when I reorganise my bookshelves, and when I read all the books that I acquired in the previous year and failed to actually read; it is also the time when I re-read beloved novels, just for the pleasure of reacquainting myself with old friends. In summer I want big, splashy ideas and trashy novels, devoured in a garden chair, or perched on one of the wave-breaks on the beach. In winter I want concepts to chew over in a pool of lamplight; slow, spiritual reading; a re-enforcement of the soul. Winter is a time for libraries: the muffled quiet of book-stacks and the scent of old pages and dust. In winter, I can spend hours in silent pursuit of a half-understood concept, or a detail of history. There is nowhere else to be, after all.

Winter opens up time: 'there is nothing doing', as Sylvia Plath notes in her poem 'Wintering'. 'This is the time of hanging on for the bees', she says, having 'whirled the midwife's extractor' to collect their honey. It's now lined up in jars – six of them – on a shelf in her cellar, while they feed on sugar syrup: 'Tate and Lyle [...] instead of flowers.' In the emptiness that winter brings, Plath huddles in her cellar, picking out the leftover possessions of former tenants in her yellow torchlight, and finding only 'Black asininity. Decay./ Possession.' She wonders if the hive will survive.

Plath, as every schoolgirl knows, did not survive her winter. She wrote 'Wintering' towards the end of her life, and it marked the end of her own draft of *Ariel*, her iconic collection of love and despair, hope and loss, before it was re-edited for publication by her husband, Ted Hughes, after her suicide. 'Wintering' takes us into the depths of darkness, in the depths of the house, 'the black bunched in there like a bat'. I always find it a difficult poem to read. Its syntax never sits quite right to my eye. Its sentences meander across lines and stanzas; its meanings blur. In it, I find a kind of disorder, as though we are dropped into the middle of a thought process whose beginning and end we can't perceive.

In Hughes's version of *Ariel*, we come, finally, to two poems that take on extra resonance after the death of their author. 'Edge', which at times seems to fetishise a demise that has already occurred, or which at least is inevitable; and then, as a coda, 'Words', which finds a kind of stillness in death; an aftermath. But this is a memorial, arranged like a wreath after the author has gone, perhaps intending to make sense of such a tragedy; perhaps, as feminist commentators have often argued, signalling Hughes's desire to control Plath's narrative even after death. Either way, Plath herself never intended this ending. As she arranged it, *Ariel* concluded on an altogether lighter note, the return of life: 'The bees are flying. They taste the spring.'

In the very depths of winter, Plath seems to reach for a way to survive through work – women's work, the kind that entails quiet hours in the house. 'Winter is for women,' she says in 'Wintering'. It is, perhaps, a time when the feminine arts come into their own; but she is also commenting, I think, on lean times that women can survive. It leaves me wishing that there was more for her to do: more honey to spin; more bees to feed.

Plath's instincts towards keeping her hands moving in the winter turned out to be correct. A 2007 study by Harvard Medical School found that knitting can lower blood pressure as much as yoga and can also help to relieve sufferers of chronic pain by releasing serotonin. In 2018, the charity Knit for Peace conducted research on the health benefits of crafting, and found that it had a range of benefits for their members, including maintaining mental sharpness, helping smokers to quit and reducing loneliness and isolation in the elderly. They went on to argue that craft should be prescribed on the NHS.

While I'm labouring through my own winter, I take up my knitting needles for the first time in years, producing a series of wonky hats that wear their dropped stitches like badges of honour. It feels good to be making something, even while my contribution to the world feels very small. It allows me to imagine I'm part machine, fluid and efficient. And while I knit, I dream of owning my own beehive one day, spinning out jars of honey and padding down the garden to my hive in midwinter, just to feel the hum of life inside.

SONG

I N THE DEEPEST OF WINTER, the robin begins to sing.
I spot our one in the garden in January, perched
on the fence next to the bay tree, head cocked, his
intelligent little eyes examining me. His breast – a rich
orange rather than red – glows like a berry against the
muted greens and browns of my dormant garden.

He's dropped by from next door to see what I'm
up to. I don't feed birds in my own backyard, because
I have three cats, and I would feel like I was setting some kind of terrible trap. My neighbour does,
though, and I sometimes get blue tits and goldfinches
straying in from her hanging feeder, probably hoping
that I'm just as generous. Best of all, I get the robin,
who seems to arrive just to be sociable.

Robins are the friendliest of birds, happy to flit
around close to gardeners in the hope of reaping the
uncovered worms. More than other birds, they seem

to have realised that we are less of a threat than a potential provider of bounty. But they also seem to feel some kind of fascination for us, watching us with a cocked head, as if asking, 'What are you doing?' History is littered with people who've felt that they've developed enduring friendships with robins that have sometimes lasted for years, although we are told that this is often an illusion created by all robins being friendly and looking the same. However, plenty of patient souls have managed to tame their garden robin. The actor Mackenzie Crook has a companion robin called Winter George. 'He would think nothing of coming into the house', wrote Crook in the *Telegraph* in 2017, 'perching on my shoulder and shouting at me while I was cooking for my family. He is brilliant and fearless.' He tamed the robin slowly as he dug his garden, first of all by throwing him worms, and eventually persuading him to take a centipede from his fingers. After that, Crook bought live mealworms from the local pet shop, and coaxed the bird to his back door. Winter George is now a permanent fixture in his household, and has bred several clutches of chicks in his garden.

Much to my regret, I have never befriended a robin, but I always see them as the cheerleaders of the bird family. They have a habit of appearing when you're at a low ebb, as if to encourage you onwards by reminding you that there is some magic left in the world. I used to run (or attempt to) down a long track between Whitstable and Canterbury, and there was a point at which I would stagger to the top of a hill and then feel as though I was good for nothing else than passing out behind the nearest tree. I would slow my pace and wonder why on earth I put myself through this, and at that moment, a robin would always appear on the path in front of me, as if to urge me on. I would gasp, 'Hello old friend,' and smile, and it was hard not to see him as a sign that I ought to push on. He would flit along the branches beside me until it was time to loop round and go home.

Robins first became strongly associated with winter in Victorian times, as the stars of the new fashion for Christmas cards. This might have been a kind of joke because the postmen who delivered them were known as 'robins' because of their red jackets. But the cards most probably refer to an earlier association with the robin and birth of Christ. One traditional fable tells that the robin got his red breast in the manger, where he had come to watch the baby Jesus. He noticed that the fire had blazed dangerously high, and placed himself between the flames and the sleeping infant. His breast was scorched to the deep red that he passed on to his descendants.

But the robin's link to Christmas may have more obvious origins too. Quite simply, the robin seems to be around at a time when other birds are not. They don't migrate, and their bright plumage and friendly habits make them more visible than other birds. And, in addition, they sing through the darkest months.

Other birds call in the winter too, but these are often defensive notes, aimed at warding off predators. Robins, however, engage in full, complex song from the very depths of the cold, when it's far too early to consider breeding. A 2002 study by John McNamara of the University of Bristol found that robins will sing as soon as the days begin to get longer, providing they have energy to spare. A well-fed robin, who has laid on sufficient fat to survive the lean winter months, and who has found a reliable source of nutrition to top up his reserves, will sing to advertise the fact well in advance of the time that he expects females to act on his display. In evolutionary biology, this is known as 'costly signalling': a gesture that advertises your superior strength and vitality which, by its very nature, is potentially dangerous to the creature. A robin sings in winter because it can, and it wants the world – or at least the female robins – to know it. But he is also practising for happier times.

★

A year after I had my son, I lost my voice. I don't mean that I lost it altogether; instead, it became weak and thin, trembling at the edges. If I spoke for any length of time, it would begin to crackle, and then cut in and out like a faulty microphone. My throat tickled. I would cough ineffectually. Eventually, it would whistle into silence, while I swallowed and drank water and fretfully tried to rest it back into life again.

I have navigated my entire life by talking, and suddenly my voice was unreliable. My speech was being chopped up, my words randomly erased. In everyday conversation with people I knew, I would talk until it faded, and then just wave my hand, hoping they could extrapolate the rest of what I meant to say. In the outside world it was more difficult. I found myself blaming colds and sore throats that I didn't have, without really knowing why I was lying. I suppose it was preferable to be seen as temporarily useless, rather than feeling permanently so. Often, in large groups of people I didn't know, I wouldn't speak at all. My voice was a busted flush. There was no point even starting. Better to stay silent than to splutter and whisper until they lost interest.

With this voicelessness coming out of the first eighteen months of motherhood, I felt like a walking metaphor. All those silent days of infancy, which are filled with nothing more than a few repeated gestures, and the sound of CBeebies in the background. All those quiet whispers in the night. Being a mother felt like becoming invisible, or perhaps semi-visible

– noticeable enough to be scolded for failing to fold your pram on a bus (how, with a baby under your arm?), or for taking up too much space on the pavement. But in yourself, now, a slightly detested creature, loose around the middle and contributing to the overpopulation of the world. Sitting around drinking coffee all day, or going out to work and neglecting your maternal duty. Either/or. It doesn't matter which you choose. You are ruined.

There were times, in those early years, when I thought that nobody would ever listen to me again; that anything important I had to say was now crushed under the weight of the bag on my shoulder, full of nappies and snacks and wipes and changes of clothes. It seemed cruel that, at this moment, my voice would also fade away, but then it seemed entirely appropriate too.

One of the greatest blows was that I could no longer sing. It's tempting to glibly write, 'Not that singing played a huge part in my life ...' but that wouldn't be true. It may not be my profession, or my ambition, but singing has sustained me for as long as I can remember, from attempting harmonies in the car with my mother, to warbling along to the radio while I cook. I sang in choirs at school and at university, my low alto knitting with the other voices. Singing with others is a kind of alchemy, an act of expansive magic in which you lose yourself and become part of a whole. I have long been reliant on the stress release of booming out half-remembered choir parts when I'm driving alone in my car.

But now my voice was somehow too insubstantial to sing. Even when I could manage a few notes without crackling or croaking, there was no richness in it anymore, no glorious volume to fill my lungs and ease apart my intercostal muscles. Singing was a breathy, wheezing experience. Worst of all, my tuning had gone. I would reach for perfectly ordinary notes, and my voice would simply slide off them, into murky tunelessness. It was like losing a part of my soul.

The usual diagnoses did not apply. I had a camera inserted into my nose and pushed down my throat, and it found nothing: no polyps, no inflammation. Nothing that could be treated or cured. I had lost my voice; that was all. It was just something that had happened, alongside all the other things that obliterated my sense of being a relevant presence in the world.

When a friend suggested singing lessons, I laughed and said that really wasn't the most important thing. After all, I had no intention of ever airing my voice in public again. It really didn't matter. But she said, no, it wasn't about singing. She thought that a good teacher could help me to nurture my voice back into health, and look after it in the future. Apparently it happens all the time in the performing arts: voices become frail and need restoring or remapping. My voice was an asset, and I should treat it in the way that other professionals did. Giving up was not an option.

I was sceptical, but also drawn towards the idea of an hour in the company of a singing teacher and a piano, a quiet room and a music stand. At that moment in time, it sounded more pampering than any spa. I sent a tentative email to a teacher, explaining that I didn't really want to learn to sing per se, but instead to learn to talk again. I was surprised that he even replied, but he seemed to find my request entirely reasonable, although he did point out that I would have to sing. I thought that I could manage that. We agreed a time and date.

In the run-up, I wondered whether I actually could manage it. Newly unable to hit a single clean note and hold it, I was embarrassed to air my singing voice in public, and particularly in a room in which decent singers came to polish their style. I felt that I needed a sparse, sterile clinic, rather than the neat living room where I found myself standing, dry-mouthed, and wishing for all the world that I could hide behind a curtain in shame while I revealed the true horror of my voice.

Philip, my tutor, struck me as a practical man. I think he knew from the start that I didn't really want to sing: not in the middle of his living-room floor, and not on a stage. So we worked through some basics, like standing and breathing. I cracked the joke (which I'm sure he'd heard a million times before) that I hopefully knew how to stand and breathe by now, but at that point, I wasn't so sure if that were true. Standing and breathing felt far too much like the behaviour of a steady, competent adult; one who had a place in the world.

So I learned to make myself stable, and to take air into my lungs. And then we tried to sing some scales. Philip played a middle C, and my voice just glanced off it, and into tunelessness.

'See,' I said. It was a lost cause.

'Try B,' said Philip.

I could sing B. The note was voice and full of air, but I could hit it, and the A below it. I worked my way down through the scale, and back up it again, and found that I could hit that C when it came after a burst of other notes. It was there; it just needed me to slide onto it sideways, rather than tackling it head-on. My middle C was in hiding.

It's a peculiar thing, to lose the note where every-one tends to begin, but there it was. From then on, my scales started with an A, or even a few notes below. We would do run-ups to my C. I could find it if I thought of it as a long jump. Sometimes, you need to take a few steps back and start somewhere else.

Over the weeks that followed, we worked on getting the clarity back in my singing voice, the volume and precision of which I'd once been so proud. I learned to engage the muscles at the base of my throat, and to imagine pulling an invisible thread forwards as I sang to keep my voice originating from my lower larynx. I learned to flow one note into another, to keep my song running like water. After my sessions, I didn't have the sore throat that I expected. I felt like a small part of my body had relaxed, and that I had expanded ever so slightly. I had sucked in the air around me, and stopped being concave, pressed inwards by life.

After a couple of lessons, we fell into conversation about how I really use my voice. I was talking all day: buffeting along my family in the morning, and then, at work, spending all day using my voice to stake my claim in this world. As the course leader of a Creative Writing degree, my voice was multitasking: seeking to inspire and enthuse in the lecture hall; to console in the privacy of my office; to find firm, immovable authority in the face of the equally immovable university bureaucracy. In the times between those moments, I was endeavouring to appear cheerful and friendly in the corridors and canteens, never allowed to nod and wave mutely as I dearly wanted to. Even in my silent moments, I was pounding through miles of email correspondence, usually with my teeth clamped together in an effort to remain clear, helpful and polite. I was like a lightbulb, always on. I was using my voice like a bludgeon, trying to force everyone else to listen.

'Do you ever read your work aloud?' asked Philip.

'Sometimes,' I said. 'Not as much as I used to.' The layers of truth hidden below that: that nobody asked me to anymore; that I no longer really enjoyed the attention, nor had the faith in my work. But that I nevertheless spent all day performing, dancing with other people's writing instead of my own, trying – sometimes in vain – to energise rooms of students who were already weighed down with their own thoughts and troubles. In teaching, you cannot walk into the room unhappy or unwilling. You must sacrifice your own energy for your students', throw your personal reluctance onto the pyre of their disinterest. You must do without the traditional pedagogic luxury of believing that the people you teach are lazy, or rude, or entitled. You do it knowing instead that they are all straining under the load of their own grief, their own fear, their own burdens of work and care. You walk into your classroom and try to entertain this mass of people just enough for them to learn something that will help to alleviate their woes in the future. I suddenly saw my voice as a funnel, into which I was cramming all this weight, and asking it to create a measured stream of words that somehow mended everything.

'Do you know *Under Milk Wood*?' asked Philip, and I said that, by coincidence, I had a brand new copy sitting on my desk back at work, ready to support somebody's dissertation. At home, poked into the towering stacks of my husband's vinyl collection, is my own copy of Richard Burton's 1954 recording of the Dylan Thomas play. As a text, I find it unknowable, but I'm always drawn to its undulating rhythms and wicked humour.

Philip opened his copy and rested it on the music stand. 'Read the first page,' he said, and all over again my voice faltered. *It is spring, moonless night in the small town, starless and bible-black, the cobblestreets silent ...* I couldn't marshal my breath for those long, meandering sentences. In silence, I could understand them well enough, but aloud, I stammered over them like a child learning to read. The first paragraph seemed to take a lifetime to unravel. My voice was like a hammer, randomly hitting at syllables and bouncing onto others, sharp and percussive.

After I'd mangled, *And all the people of the lulled and dumfound town are sleeping now*, Philip stopped me. 'Listen,' he said, and he read it himself, bouncing softly onto each stressed syllable, letting the words wash over each other like waves on the sea. 'You have to approach it like a song,' he said. 'Take your time. Don't attack it. Roll along with it.'

I tried again, shy this time, now that I'd seen my own flaws so clearly. This was something I thought I knew: how to read aloud, and read well. But I hadn't read this gentle, flowing text so much as dismantled it. I had gone at it like a thing to be conquered, and instead it had conquered me. I took a breath. *It is spring …*

I was slower now, and found a little more meaning, but I still felt as though I was caught up in a three-way fight between my brain, my breath and this stubbornly languid text. It was shining a light on everything that was wrong in my life at that moment in time: the way that I was locked in an attack on my immediate environment, rather than merging into it. The way that I could not match the ambulatory pace of the play, either in the confines of a music lesson or outside of it.

'Long Welsh vowels,' said Philip, and that made things a little better. It was hard to elongate my own, clipped Kentish phrasing without pastiching the accent, but we practised individual words and the unhurried tone gradually fell into place: *hymning in bonnet and brooch and bombazine black*, that final *k* clicking like a wet log on a warm fire. I read the line, *trotting silent, with seaweed on its hooves, along the cockled cobbles*, and it was a kind of revelation: the whole play rolls along over cobblestones on which it is impossible to rush.

Listen. It is night moving in the streets … Listen. It is night in the chill, squat chapel. When you start to use your voice as music, you are allowed to demand attention; you are allowed to say, 'Listen.' My voice had waned alongside my confidence, and asserting it again was like asserting my rightful part in the adult world. I was gabbling out my words because I felt I had to get them in before I was interrupted.

My own voice had already gone through so many changes. As a child, I was praised when I 'spoke nicely', and told off whenever I dropped my 't's to mimic the estuary English that I heard all around me in my native Gravesend. This precise way of speaking went down well at my primary school, although I often had to be corrected when, in reception class, I repeatedly tried to absorb my teacher's Yorkshire accent. Moving to a council estate aged eight, the other kids mocked my poshness, so I tried to talk more like them, only to be corrected when I got back home. I modified my voice again and again, at home and at school. It was like being a tennis ball: at one end of the court, my voice was one thing; at the other end, it quickly had to become the opposite.

At my grammar school in Rochester, filled with girls who had passed their Eleven Plus in the local crammer, and whose fathers were doctors and solicitors, my voice shifted again. For the first time in my life, I felt how poor we were, and seethed in embarrassment when I knew we couldn't meet the financial demands of this state school that thought it was more. When new blazers were demanded, or jumpers with stripes around the neck, or expensive art materials to prop up the supplies in class, I would dig in my heels and use my voice to point out how common I was. That talk I'd learned from the kids on my estate – which was never my own – became suddenly useful. I couldn't pretend to be like the other girls, so I became something deliberately different, defiantly rough around the edges. When I was challenged about the uniform violation – the wrong skirt, the wrong shoes – I learned that the teachers would shrink away if I raised my voice and said, 'We can't afford the proper ones,' or, better still, 'I bought it in a charity shop.' I found my power in the fluster that is caused by asserting that you have less than other people. If grammar school was supposed to turn me into a nice young lady, it actually turned me into an urchin.

At university, my voice changed again, immersed as it was in the clipped tones of the truly posh. I could have gone either way – full R. P. or full Estuary – but I didn't have the heart for either, so instead I spoke more quietly, and tried my best to pronounce my consonants clearly. Back home in the holidays, it was pointed out that university had changed me; that I had got a little above myself. And so on, and so on. My voice is now a chameleon, changing to suit whoever I'm talking to. I don't even notice myself doing it anymore, except in those moments of terrible cognitive dissonance, when I am forced to speak to people from two disparate parts of my life at once. Then, unable to imitate either, I have to consciously tread a middle path, and it's horrible.

Women's voices are always contested in a way that men's never are. If we speak too softly, we are treated as gentle mice; if we raise our voices to be heard, we are shrill. Margaret Thatcher famously had elocution lessons at the beginning of her political career in order to project more authority. Her advisor, the former television producer Gordon Reece, got rid of her hard hairdo and fussy clothes, and guided her towards a lower, more certain voice, its plumminess removed in favour of something more ordinary, harder to place in the class system. Thatcher worked with a coach from the National Theatre to breathe correctly and to slow down her phrasing, and was not allowed to sound confrontational or aggressive. Instead, she had to adopt the intimate tones of the mother or nanny, gently encouraging us towards her decisions with firm certainty, or the lover, whispering her power across a pillow. Her voice had to carry the weight of the nation's fear of women, and make them believe that we could think straight. Her voice was not allowed to confront the patriarchy head-on; instead, it had to coerce and cajole it into sense with its words, all the while assuring it that women were housewives and mothers, and that Thatcher was just an unusual outcrop of that natural female tendency; not a threat, but merely a useful tool to attract a group of voters who were electorally important, but culturally insignificant: women.

Never having stood for election myself, I had still somehow modified my voice like Thatcher did, softening it to remove its threat, and learning to disrupt its natural stridency and fluency. People used to complain that I talked at them instead of to them, and so I discovered that I could inflect my sentences with moments of mock-hesitation, adding in *ums* and *ers* to appear more uncertain than I actually felt. Now, standing in this room with the rain hammering on the window, I let my voice find its fluency again, absorbing myself in the pleasure of my own speech, the way that my throat could fill with the resonance of my voice.

Within four lessons, I had remapped it, bringing it lower and louder and softer and slower. I had learned to almost sing my words, to let them elide into each other as a continuous river of notes, like birdsong. My middle C reappeared, but that didn't seem like the most important gain. My crackle had gone. When I spoke now, my voice felt smooth and slick, as though it had been oiled. It no longer tickled; it no longer broke. The words flowed back out of me, like silk.

But I was glad to sing again, too. It had been a greater loss than I'd realised, in that particular wintering which saw the waning of my voice. It wasn't about the vanity of being able to trill out a fine song; it was about the joy of singing for its own sake. In twenty-first-century Britain, we've linked singing with talent, and we've got that fundamentally wrong. The right to sing is an absolute, regardless of how it sounds to the outside world. We sing because we must. We sing because it fills our lungs with nourishing air, and lets our heart soar with the notes we let out. We sing because it allows us to speak of love and loss, delight and desire, all encoded in lyrics that let us pretend that those feelings are not quite ours. In song, we have permission to rehearse all our heartbreaks, all our lusts. In song, we can console our children while they are still too young to judge our rusty voices, and we can find shortcuts to ecstasy while performing the mundane duty of a daily shower, or scrubbing down the kitchen after yet another meal.

Best of all, we can sing together, whole families knowing the same songs and giving them the same meaning. When I sing with my mother, I am struck every time that our voices are the same. There's a moment of deep, genetic resonance in hitting the exact same note, in the exact same way. When I sing with my husband, our voices clash, but we sing the songs that mean something only to us, most often the yearning tones of the song 'Wichita Lineman'. When I sing with my son, I am teaching him something: not just words and lyrics, but how to survive. Like the robin, we sometimes sing to show how strong we are, and sometimes sing in hope of better times. We sing either way.

EPILOGUE: LATE MARCH

THAW

EVERY MORNING, I DRIVE PAST a buzzard sitting on the fence by Manston Airport. He's enormous and grizzled, the feathers on his breast in permanent disarray. I like to think that he's lived a little, and that he sits here to proudly display his war wounds. Here he is this morning, a lone sentry. I just about catch the yellow of his beak as I flash past. I'm beginning to think he waits here for me. He's my totem, the anchor to my day. He quells the anxious storm in my gut. He's there. I feel as though he witnesses me.

I want this all to end like a neat narrative arc should: life is settled again, certain; all my problems solved; all my worries resolved. I want Bert to be happily installed in a new school that's a perfect fit for him, or for us to have decided to abandon the idea of school altogether, and to gloriously, bravely, stride out into the world alone. I want to be able to say that we are not wondering whether, on balance, we should sell our house and move to somewhere smaller, in a cheaper town. I would like to say that I do not still routinely joke that we should probably move into that caravan in the woods, because that's the only thing we could reliably afford. Instead, I am often taut with worry, and sometimes feel as though we're only a footstep away from chaos. But I have to hold my nerve, for fear of passing on my chronic sense of unbelonging in this world. I don't feel up to the task. I wonder, for the thousandth time this year, whether I'm good enough.

I take a walk around Pegwell Bay to clear my head. Winter is on its way out. Only a week ago, we woke to find the surrounding fields pale with frost and the edge of every leaf picked out in white. Today is one of those voluminous days that feel like spring, with enormous blue skies strewn with clouds, and playful blasts of wind that are almost warm. There are clumps of snowdrops along the path, and catkins dangling lime green from the hazel. The marshes were frozen solid only a few days ago, but now they are flowing and lapping and rippling, waded by little egrets and sifted by curlews. I am told that you can see seals lazing around at the mouth of the creek. My luck isn't in today. I promise myself that I will remember my binoculars the next time I come.

As I walk, I remind myself of the words of Alan Watts: 'To hold your breath is to lose your breath.' In *The Wisdom of Insecurity*, Watts makes a case that always convinces me, but which I always seem to forget: that life is, by nature, uncontrollable. That we should stop trying to finalise our comfort and security somehow, and instead find a radical acceptance of the endless, unpredictable change that is the very essence of this life. Our suffering, he says, comes from the fight we put up against this fundamental truth: 'Running away from fear is fear, fighting pain is pain, trying to be brave is being scared. If the mind is in pain, the mind is in pain. The thinker has no other form than his thought. There is no escape.'

For Watts, the only moment we can depend on is the present: that which we know and sense right now. The past is gone. The future, to which we devote so much of our brainpower, is an unstable element, entirely unknowable; 'a will-o'-the-wisp that ever eludes our grasp'. When we endlessly ruminate over these distant times, we miss extraordinary things in the present moment. They are, in actual fact, all we have: the here and now; the direct perception of our senses. Whenever I return to Watts's work, a small, rebellious voice rises up in me and shouts: *That's not fair! Life is more secure for some people than for others!* But that doesn't make it any less true. Watts isn't offering us a cheap, puffed-up solution to the vagaries of life; he isn't telling us that, if we can only master this small trick of thought, all our dreams will come to fruition. He is telling us the truth. Change will not stop happening. The only part we can control is our response.

Some ideas are too big to take in once and completely. For me, this is one of them. Believing in the unpredictability of my place on this earth – radically and deeply accepting it to be true – is something I can only do in glimpses. It is, in itself, an exercise in mindfulness. I remind myself of its force, but the belief soon seeps away. I remind myself again. It drifts off with the tide. This does nothing to diminish the power of the next realisation, and the next. I am willing to do it over and over again, throughout my life. I am willing to accept that it may never actually stick, but that it's no less essential.

I catch a movement in the air, and I turn to see a flock of birds, all rolling together at the edge of the sea. At first, I think they're a murmuration of starlings, but even from here I can tell they're too large. Rooks? There's a rookery less than a mile from here, where many times I have watched the mass of rippling forms rise collectively from a pair of trees. It's an astonishing sight, but not the same.

They are getting closer. I realise that my arms have dropped to my sides and I am standing stock-still, gazing up at them. There is no happiness greater than this. Every part of me is absorbed in this moment: their extraordinary flow; the silent decisions that govern their turns. For a moment, the group loses its coherence and they scatter, black polka dots spacing out across the sky. It is as if they are water, and they have splashed. One flies overhead, and then another: a white body with black wings, rounded at the tips. Lapwing. I have never seen so many before. I never knew they could do this.

★

I've noticed lately a glut of posts on Facebook offering unsolicited advice on how to cope with a crisis: *Hang on in there!* they say, apropos of nothing. *You are stronger than you know.* They are presented like greetings cards, pastel text on dreamy backgrounds, the words rendered in elegant cursive as though scrawled by a particularly inspirational friend. Reading them, I always assume that they're aimed at someone in particular; that the person who posted them has noticed some hint of distress and is sending out an oblique message of support. Either that or it's a cry for help, a signal pitched into the ether to come back to its originator, like talking to yourself.

This is where we are now: endlessly cheerleading ourselves into positivity, while erasing the dirty underside of real life. I always read brutality in those messages: they offer next to nothing. There are days when I can say, with great certainty, that I am *not* strong enough to manage. And what if I can't hang on in there? What then? These people might as well be leaning into my face, shouting, *Cope! Cope! Cope!* while spraying perfume into the air to make it all seem nice. The subtext of these messages is clear: misery is not an option. We must carry on looking jolly for the sake of the crowd. While we may no longer see depression as a failure, we expect you to spin it into something meaningful pretty quick. We don't have the answers, after all. And if you can't pull that off, then you'd better disappear from view for a while. You're dragging down the vibe.

This is the opposite of caring. I've never believed – as others do – that social media is a place entirely constructed of fake lives and fake friendships, but I do think it's another place to beware. There's a collector's mentality online; our social worth is given a single, blunt number. We have to make sure that we're not fooled by it. We have to make the same assessments that we always did about the quality of those connections, their individual meanings to us and the nurture that they can realistically offer us. Just as with the physical world, many of these friends will melt away at the first sign of trouble. The only difference is that the numbers are bigger online, and our missed connections feel more visible.

I'm beginning to think that unhappiness is one of the simple things in life: a pure, basic emotion to be respected, if not savoured. I would never dream of suggesting that we should wallow in misery, or shrink from doing everything we can to alleviate it; but I do think it's instructive. After all, unhappiness has a function: it tells us that something is going wrong. If we don't allow ourselves the fundamental honesty of our own sadness, then we miss an important cue to adapt. We seem to be living in an age when we're bombarded with entreaties to be happy, but we're suffering from an avalanche of depression; we're urged to stop sweating the small stuff, and yet we're chronically anxious. I often wonder if these are just normal feelings that become monstrous when they're denied. A great deal of life will always suck. There will be moments when we're riding high, and moments when we can't bear to get out of bed. Both are normal. Both, in fact, require a little perspective.

Sometimes, the best response to our howls of anguish is the honest one: we need friends who wince along with our pain, who tolerate our gloom, and who allow us to be weak for a while when we're finding our feet again. We need people who acknowledge that we can't always hang on in there; that sometimes, everything breaks. Short of that, we need to perform those functions for ourselves: to give ourselves a break when we need it, and to be kind. To find our own grit, in our own time.

When I set out to write this book, I fully intended to do more. I meant to travel the world in pursuit of winter, to visit locations that felt truly exotic to me, and to interview people whom I considered to have wintered in extreme ways. I thought that I'd find greater wisdom there than I could have found in my own back yard. I also thought that I could snatch a moment to write about wintering while I was in between winters; that I could use the momentum of the good times to prise apart the bad.

But in the process, life happened. Life happened a great deal, actually. As if I'd ineptly summoned them, several winters came at once. My world shrank, literally and metaphorically. I couldn't do as much as I'd hoped. I couldn't be the person I'd imagined: cheerful, energetic, summery. In fact, I struggled. I was dragged under by periods of depression. I was gnawed at by anxiety. There were times when I thought that I probably couldn't write this; that I wasn't up to it; that doing so would bring about some kind of catastrophe of embarrassment, just for having the guile to think I had anything to say on the matter. Once upon a time, this would have engulfed me entirely for a season, and I would have emerged in a year or two, shaking my head and starting again.

But here I am, and here it is. The only difference – the only reason I have finished this – is experience. I recognised winter. I saw it coming (a mile off, since you ask), and I looked it in the eye. I greeted it, and let it in. I had some tricks up my sleeve, you see. I've learned them the hard way. When I started feeling the drag of winter, I began to treat myself like a favoured child: with kindness and love. I assumed my needs were reasonable, and that my feelings were signals of something important. I kept myself well fed, and made sure I was getting enough sleep. I took myself for walks in the fresh air, and spent time doing things that soothed me. I asked myself: what is this winter all about? I asked myself: what change is coming?

At its base, this is not a book about beauty, but about reality. It is about noticing what's going on, and living it. That's what the natural world does: it carries on surviving. Sometimes it flourishes – lays on fat, garlands itself in leaves, makes abundant honey – and sometimes it pares back to the very basics of exist-ence in order to keep living. It doesn't do this once, resentfully, assuming that one day it will get things right and everything will smooth out. It winters in cycles, again and again, forever and ever. For plants and animals, winter is part of the job. The same is true for humans.

To get better at wintering, we need to address our very notion of time. We tend to imagine that our lives are linear, but they are in fact cyclical. I would not, of course, seek to deny that we grow gradually older, but while doing so, we pass through phases of good health and ill, of optimism and deep doubt, of freedom and constraint. There are times when everything seems easy, and times when it all seems impossibly hard. To make that manageable, we only have to remember that our present will one day become a past, and our future will be our present. We know that, because it's happened before. The things we put behind us will often come around again. The things that trouble us now will one day be past history. Each time we endure the cycle, we ratchet up a notch. We learn from the last time around, and we do a few things better this time; we develop tricks of the mind to see us through. This is how progress is made. But one thing is certain: we will simply have different things to worry about. We will have to clench our teeth and carry on surviving again.

In the meantime, we can only deal with what's in front of us at this moment in time. We take the next necessary action, and the next. At some point along the line, that next action will feel joyful again.

★

A year after I left my job, I finally sorted through all the books that I'd brought home from my office. At first, they had sat there as a desolate reminder of something that I no longer was; a fleeting vision of myself that I had failed to make real. After a while, I forgot they were there, and they became part of the general clutter of my study.

By the time I got round to really looking at them, they had lost something of their potency. My old identity had passed, unmourned. The guilt had gone. I had walked away from something which, in retrospect, was toxic to me. I picked up each book in turn, sometimes in fond recognition, sometimes in contempt. Many of them drew a blank in my mind: were they really mine? What business could I possibly have had with them? I was happy to pile a load of them into carrier bags, and haul them down to the nearest charity shop.

Others found a home on my shelves, where they nestled amongst my personal collection. I had to re-arrange the whole bookcase to fit them in, stacking everything sideways to make more space. One day, I will need a whole library, but for now I have just about enough shelves, as long as I don't buy any more. This is a resolution that I know I won't keep. Next year, and the year after, and the year after that, I will have to give more away. I rather like that notion. At the moment, there are yards of books that I'm saving simply so that Bert will be able to put his hand to them when he's a little older, before he starts forming a collection of his own. There will come a time when there's no longer any point in clinging on to them, and I'll be able to whittle them down to the kernel of what I truly love. It will be like shedding a skin.

Spring cleaning is an instinctive response to the end of winter. The Gaelic festival of Imbolc is held on the first day of February, and is associated with dusting away the cobwebs that have grown in the corners during the darkest months. In contemporary Ireland, it is still often marked as St Brigid's Day – a Christianis-ation of the feast of that ancient goddess Brighde, who is now stirring, ready to take over from the winter goddess, the Cailleach. Brighde is all promise and life, bursting with readiness to bring about change. She is well rested after her winter retreat.

Like Brighde, we must emerge slowly from our wintering. We must test the air and be ready to shrink back into safety when blasted by unseasonal winds; we must gradually unfurl our new leaves. There will still often be the debris to shift of a long, disordered season. These are the moments when we have to find the most grace: when we come to atone for the worst ravages of our conduct in darker times; when we have to tell truths that we'd rather ignore. Sometimes, we will have to name our personal winters, and the words will feel barbed in our throats: grief, rejection, depression, illness. Shame, failure, despair.

It often seems easier to stay in winter, burrowed down into our hibernation nests, away from the glare of the sun. But we are brave, and the new world awaits us, gleaming and green, alive with the beat of wings. And besides, we have a kind of gospel to tell now, and a duty to share it. We who have wintered have learned some things. We sing it out like birds. We let our voices fill the air.

ACKNOWLEDGEMENTS

THIS BOOK IS THE WORK of many hands, and I only hope I can remember to thank them all.

First and foremost, thanks to my interviewees, who were extremely generous with their time and their willingness to explore some difficult subjects. Any errors are mine and not theirs. Thanks also to Richard Ashcroft for emergency philosophical consultation services.

Thanks to Nira Begum, Olivia Morris, Bianca Bexton, Sue Lascelles and the brilliant team at Rider Books; and to Anna Hogarty, Hayley Steed, Madeleine Milburn and the Madeleine Milburn Literary, TV and Film Agency. It's hard to express my gratitude and surprise each time one of my book ideas is taken seriously and treated with such care.

Thanks to all the friends and family who rushed in to help during a difficult couple of years. Thanks to H for finding many ingenious ways to allow me to sneak off and write, and to Lucy Abrahams for discreetly diverting work away from me so that I could finish my manuscript. She probably thinks I didn't notice.

Finally, thanks to Bert for constantly forcing me to dig deep into this life. It's always worth it.